Your Catholic Wedding

A COMPLETE PLANBOOK

Revised and Updated

CHRIS ARIDAS

A Crossroad Book
THE CROSSROAD PUBLISHING COMPANY
NEW YORK

This printing: 2000

The Crossroad Publishing Company
370 Lexington Avenue, New York, NY 10017

Printed in the United States of America

Library of Congress Cataloging-in-Publication Data

Aridas, Chris, 1947-
Your Catholic wedding: a complete plan-book / Chris Aridas.
p. cm.
"Revised and updated."
Originally published: Doubleday Anchor, 1982.
ISBN 0-8245-1675-3 (pbk.)
1. Marriage—religious aspects—Catholic Church. 2. Marriage service. 3. Wedding etiquette. 4. Catholic Church—Liturgy—Texts. I. Title.
BX2250.A57 1997
265'.5—dc21 97-565
CIP

To my parents, whose commitment
to each other in the Sacrament of Marriage
has shown me the depth of life that is
possible for those who are willing to love.

CONTENTS

Dear friends in Christ: As you know, you are about to enter into a union which is most sacred and most serious, a union which was established by God himself. By it, he gave to man a share in the greatest work of creation, the work of the continuation of the human race. And in this way he sanctified human love and enabled man and woman to help each other live as children of God by sharing a common life under his fatherly care.

Because God himself is thus its author, marriage is of its very nature a holy institution, requiring of those who enter into it a complete and unreserved giving of self. But Christ our Lord added to the holiness of marriage an even deeper meaning and a higher beauty. He referred to the love of marriage to describe his own love for his Church, that is, for the people of God whom he redeemed by his own blood. And so he gave to Christians a new vision of what married life ought to be, a life of self-sacrificing love like his own. It is for this reason that his apostle, St. Paul, clearly states that marriage is now and for all time to be considered a great mystery, intimately bound up with the supernatural union of Christ and the Church, which union is also to be its pattern.

This union, then, is most serious, because it will bind you together for life in a relationship so close and so intimate that it will profoundly influence your whole future. That future, with its hopes and disappointments, its successes and its failures, its pleasures and its pains, its joys and its sorrows, is hidden from your eyes. You know that these elements are mingled in every life and are to be expected in your own. And so, not knowing what is before you, you take each other for better or for worse, for richer or for poorer, in sickness and in health, until death.

Truly, then these words are most serious. It is a beautiful tribute to your undoubted faith in each other, that, recognizing their full import, you are nevertheless so willing and ready to pronounce them. And because these words involve such solemn obligations, it is most fitting that you rest the security of your wedded life upon the great principle of self-sacrifice. And so you begin your married life by the voluntary and complete surrender of your individual lives in the interest of that deeper and wider life which you are to have in common. Henceforth you belong entirely to each other; you will be one in mind, one in heart, and one in affections. And whatever sacrifices you may hereafter be required to make to preserve this common life, always make them generously. Sacrifice is usually difficult and irksome. Only love can make it easy; and perfect love can make it a joy. We are willing to give in proportion as we love. And when love is perfect, the sacrifice is complete. God so loved the world that he gave his only begotten Son, and the Son so loved us that he gave himself for our salvation. "Greater love than this no one has, that one lay down his life for his friends."

No greater blessing can come to your married life than pure conjugal love, loyal and true to the end. May, then, this love with which you join your hands and hearts today never fail, but grow deeper and stronger as the years go on. And if true love and the unselfish spirit of perfect sacrifice guide your every action, you can expect the greatest measure of earthly happiness that may be allotted to man in this vale of tears. The rest is in the hands of God. Nor will God be wanting to your needs: he will pledge you the life-long support of his graces in the holy sacrament which you are now going to receive.

Exhortation Before Marriage
Taken from the Old Roman Ritual

Preface to the Updated Edition

You've decided on the date. Excitement is building. Plans are underway: the church, the reception, the bridal party. On and on it goes—lists, directions, dreams not yet dreamt. For some, a maze of confusion; for others, a time of numbing joy. Many are overwhelmed by it all, yet it remains as part of the excitement itself. A seeming contradiction: confusion, yet joy.

And so this book appears. The author hopes it will help you wind your way through the labyrinth of details, questions, and preparations which engaged couples usually encounter. There's so much to think of: the liturgy, the reception, the parties before and after. What a shame if the hectic pace of the preparations deprived you of the joy that should be yours! What a loss if you lose focus because everything keeps getting out of focus!

It was with this in mind that *Your Catholic Wedding* was first written. Since then, this user-friendly guide has helped more than one hundred thousand couples raise the right questions, prepare the right lists, and find the right "rhythm" so their wedding preparations might be a joy and not a burden. Hopefully, you will find this new edition a helpful guide as well.

At this point you may ask, "What can an unmarried priest tell me regarding marriage preparations? After all, he's never done it!" Your observation, of course, is true; your conclusion, however, is incorrect. You see, most clergy have assisted in countless weddings, thereby gaining a great deal of practical information and "experience" which can assist you. Rather than sailing an uncharted course, therefore, you will be sharing and learning from the experiences of many who have gone through this time of preparation. Read on and see if you don't agree.

Introduction

What To Expect from *Your Catholic Wedding*

An important part of your preparation will be the time you spend together discussing your understanding and the Church's understanding of the Sacrament of Marriage. Quite frankly, it is not unusual for the couple to be misinformed or uninformed. It often happens that the couple simply assumes that they will receive the Sacrament.

This book should help you raise the proper questions, not in the way that a parish or diocesan Pre-Cana conference might, but rather as an opportunity for you to reflect on your decision to receive the Sacrament in the Church.

In addition, *Your Catholic Wedding* will provide the information you need to plan your wedding ceremony and to prepare for the secular celebration that usually follows.

Please do not look for a systematic or scholarly reflection on the nature of the Sacrament. For priests and couples who desire such a treatment, other authors should be consulted.*

---

* Bernard J. Cooke, *Christian Sacraments and Christian Personality* (New York: Holt, Rinehart and Winston, 1965). John Haughey, *Should Anyone Say Forever?* (Garden City, New York: Doubleday Image, 1975). Rosemary Haughton, *The Theology of Marriage* (Notre Dame, Indiana: Fides Publication, 1971). Michael G. Lawler, *Marriage and Sacrament: A Theology of Christian Marriage* Collegeville, Minnesota: The Liturgical Press, 1993). Edward Schillebeeckx, *Marriage: Human Reality and Saving Mystery* (New York: Sheed & Ward, 1965). Alexander Schemann, *For the Life of the Word: Sacraments and Orthodoxy* (Crestwood, New York: St. Vladimir's Seminary Press, 1973). Kenneth W. Stevenson, *To Join Together: The Rite of Marriage* (New York: Pueblo Publishing Company, 1987).

How To Use This Book

The first chapter of *Your Catholic Wedding* will give an overview of the Sacrament itself. The proper context will be described; questions will be raised. The second chapter will discuss the initial church arrangements, leading to a discussion of the marriage ceremony itself in the third chapter.

The fourth chapter outlines the Rite of Marriage, the fifth gives Scripture passages and reflections, while the sixth and final chapter is a series of lists providing some practical and helpful hints to assist you as you "order the confusion" of the wedding preparations. Found within this section is a detachable form which can be filled out and given to the priest/deacon officiating at the wedding. In this way your own personal record remains intact.

An important attitude to maintain during this time of preparation is one of openness—to surprise, to questions, to disappointment, to growth and reflection, to conversion. Your willingness to work toward this attitude individually and as a couple will guarantee a fruitful preparation experience.

During this time (indeed, during your entire married life) do not be satisfied with our society's notions or expectations regarding marriage. The Sacrament you will share is an adventure, an enterprise in grace not readily supported by our culture. Rather, it is founded and supported in the love you have for the Lord who manifests and reveals himself to you through each other within the Christian community. That "notion" does not exist in our world; it exists only in the hearts of those who believe.

Finally, "think big," for it is the Lord who calls you together, to reveal Himself to you in a new and vibrant way. Expect it to be so.

One

THE SACRAMENT

As an engaged couple approaching the Church for marriage, it is important for each of you to ask a basic, though difficult question: "Why am I getting married in the Church?" You may be surprised that I place this question above all others, yet, experience has shown that engaged couples seldom consider the true meaning of the Sacrament as it is revealed in Scripture and understood by the Church. More often than not, they "accept" the subtle, unspoken pressures of family and cultural upbringing without ever truly *choosing* to receive the Sacrament.

In speaking of the Sacrament's meaning, therefore, I do not wish to direct your thoughts toward rules and regulations. These are secondary to the basic question of belief and how you can live that belief in today's world.

In short, it is not enough for you to say, "I love God" or "I've always planned on being married in the Church" or "I want God to bless my wedding" or "I believe in God." These are understandable feelings and attitudes—many of them deeply ingrained through family ties and education—but they do not take us to the root question, namely, "Is Jesus alive for me, and have I begun to be alive in Him?" for without Jesus there is no Sacrament of Marriage.

ALIVE IN HIM?

I would simply be throwing words at you if, at this point, I did not offer some "sign posts" or signals which might help you take seriously the above statement. Possibly the phrases "Jesus alive in me" and "to be alive in Him" carry little or no concrete experience for your life. They are simply words that you accept, but words that do not touch your inner being. In order to bridge this gap, therefore, I would like you to consider your own relationship with your fiancé(e).

Ask yourself this question: "What has allowed me the opportunity to conclude, 'I know and love (N.)——?'" Though it may not be apparent to you at first, there are sundry experiences upon which you relied to answer the above question in a sincere and truthful way. From the many available to us, I would like to suggest four: time, dialogue, gestures of affection, and desire.

Time. A simple fact—if you had not spent time with one another, you would not have gotten to know one another. This "spending time" is done in several ways: time alone and time with others. Should you lose the balance between these two ways, you will have a partial view of your fiancé(e) rather than the deeper and more complete view needed for marriage.

The same holds true in your relationship with the Lord. Time is needed for you both to be present to Him alone (private prayer) and with others (community prayer). In order to respond to the call of love from your fiancé(e) or from the Lord, this time-to-be-present is essential. Without it, love cannot grow.

Dialogue. In your relationship with one another, you have probably realized that dialogue or sharing does not always mean words. In a deep dialogue of love, time spent together can be quiet and silent, when heart speaks to heart in wordless phrases. A dialogue that is always verbal often covers deep feelings; it can be used as a smoke screen which hides the inner person.

Our dialogue with the Lord is prayer—sometimes verbal, sometimes silent. Both alone and together this dialogue should be nurtured and experienced. In the Scripture section of this book (pages 57 ff.), I offer a helpful tool which will enable you and your fiancé(e) to enter into this type of dialogue with the Lord as a couple. Do not forget, however, to converse with Him alone in private prayer. The books listed below should help you begin or continue in this area.*

Gestures of Affection. Can you imagine a love relationship which excludes the sense of touch? A love relationship without the embrace or the kiss? Without gestures of affection, an otherwise normal love relationship might become cold, sterile, and questionable. Would you, for example, remain close to your fiancé(e) if these elements were missing? Probably not.

The same is true with the Lord. His gestures of affection, His kiss and embrace are the Sacraments where He willingly and unceasingly draws us into His life. Our gesture of affection emerges when we respond to His call by accepting Him into our lives and sharing our lives with one another. To continually turn away from His attempts to embrace us through the Sacraments is similar to your turning away from the kiss and embrace offered by your fiancé(e).

Desire. There have been times in your relationship when you were not with your fiancé(e). Though work, school,

*Edward Farrell, *Prayer Is a Hunger* (Denville, N.J.: Dimension Books, 1972). Thomas Green, *Opening to God* (Notre Dame, Ind.: Ave Maria Press, 1977). M. Basil Pennington, *Daily We Touch Him*, (Garden City: Image Books, 1979). David Rosage, *Speak, Lord, Your Servant Is Listening* (Ann Arbor, Mich.: Servant Publications, 1977). Chris Aridas, *Soundings* (Garden City: Image Books, 1984)

travel, etc., kept you apart, your desire to be with the other probably remained. More than likely, you fed the flame of desire by calling to mind and heart the image or memory of your fiancé(e). This recollection allowed you to be present to each other in a way that only love can describe.

And so with the Lord. Being "alive in Him" implies that we frequently call Him to mind so that we can be united in love through desire, just as a man and a woman are united together through their desire to be with and for the other. In this experience of love-united-by-desire, externals such as distance or time are not a barrier to union.

In reflecting on these ideas, do not get discouraged if your response right now seems vague or halfhearted. See your present situation not as a condemnation, but as an opportunity to grow into a new relationship with the Lord or to reestablish with the Lord the relationship that might have been in the past. You have here a graced moment which can return you to the true center of life and love.

Now is the time for you to reevaluate your understanding of the Gospel and your own response-ability toward Christ and His Church. Here are some questions which may help your reflection:

1. Am I praying with the Church community?
2. Am I striving to know the Lord's Gospel?
3. Am I aware of the Sacraments and how they are meant to be part of my life?

These and similar questions should be raised *before* you receive the Sacrament of Marriage.

Always remember that a "perfect response" is not necessary. What is important, however, is a response that is thoughtful, honest, and sincere. Realize that, at this point in your life, the best and most honest response may be "No".

Remember also that your response may not be the same as your fiancé(e)'s. True love, however, will affirm the other as one seeks the truth in his/her relationship with the Lord.

Your parish priest will be of assistance as you strive to do the best you are able. Far better for you to be challenged now in your faith than to live in the limbo of non-reflection into which many couples fall.

THE SACRAMENT AS GRACE FOR THE COMMUNITY

When you ask these questions, it will be important for you to understand how the Church views the Sacrament, since it is the Church which celebrates the Sacrament with you. It cannot be viewed in isolation. The Sacrament is more than two people pledging love to each other. It is a signification and sharing in the mystery of that unity and fruitful love which exists between Christ and His Church. This union of man and woman is given the dignity of a Sacrament so that "it might more clearly recall, and more easily reflect Christ's own unbreakable union with His Church."†

As a communal event, therefore, Marriage is an expression of a people's inner experience of Christ's love as it is symbolized and ritualized in the union of two members, male and female. The idea that the Sacrament is merely a blessing from God upon the couple getting married is an incomplete notion and understanding of the Sacrament.

The question now, therefore, is not whether God will bless the couple who is receiving the Sacrament. The question is whether this couple will be a source of grace and blessing for the Church community.

With this in mind, you can see why it is important for at least one of the individuals to follow the Lord within the Church. Without that movement of faith it would be impossible to be that symbol, that blessing, that grace for others. This is why the Lord is so essential and why the Church is so important. St. Paul says it best in *Ephesians* 5:21–33:

Give way to one another in obedience to Christ. Wives

† Rite of Marriage #2.

should regard their husbands as they regard the Lord, since as Christ is head of the Church and saves the whole body, so is the husband the head of his wife; and as the Church submits to Christ, so should wives to their husbands, in everything. Husbands should love their wives just as Christ loved the Church and sacrificed himself for her to make her holy. He made her clean by washing her in water with a form of words, so that when he took her to himself she would be glorious, with no speck or wrinkle or anything like that, but holy and faultless. In the same way, husbands must love their wives as they love their own bodies; for a man to love his wife is for him to love himself. A man never hates his own body, but he feeds it and looks after it; and that is the way Christ treats the Church, because it is his body—and we are its living parts. For this reason, a man must leave his father and mother and be joined to his wife, and the two will become one body. This mystery has many implications; but I am saying it applies to Christ and the Church. To sum up; you too, each one of you, must love his wife as he loves himself; and let every wife respect her husband.

THE SACRAMENT AS GRACE FOR THE COUPLE

In addition to its communal nature, the Sacrament of Marriage is also meant to grace the couple. This occurs in many ways, several of which are offered here:‡

1. The Sacrament of Marriage allows the couple to reflect and be Jesus' love for the other. As a vessel of God's love, the spouse becomes a sign, an indicator of how God is present to be "heard . . . seen with our own eyes . . .

‡ These reflections are taken from an article in *Kairos,* Vol. I, No. 11 (February 1974). The authors are Doug and Patti Michaud.

touched with our hands" (1 John 1:1). The love of each partner is meant to capture something of the way Christ loves us. Through a glance or a word, in trial or joy, the Lord's presence in love can be known now because the partner "knows" the heart of the spouse.

Just as the Word and the Eucharist are vehicles of truth for God's people, so is each partner meant to be a vehicle whereby God can touch, teach, perfect, and heal the other.

2. The Sacrament of Marriage allows each partner to know he or she is loved by God. Before we chose God, He chose us; before we knew Him, He knew us intimately, beyond our ability to see or imagine. Within the Sacrament of Marriage you and your fiancé(e) will help each other realize the very cornerstone of your existence, namely, if you can love, if you can know truth and witness to it with courage, it is because you have been known and loved by God. Through your partner, you will be reminded that from conception, and even before all time, there was One who has known you and loved you.

3. The Sacrament of Marriage allows each partner to come to know God. In the Sacrament each partner can touch the character of God's love as the Word Incarnate operates through the Lord present in the other. In the busy-ness, the high-pressured pace, when the one brings the other a rose or beckons the other to see a sunset or leads the other away from the turmoil of the day into the stillness of love's embrace, it is the Lord whom you come to know. In the strength of love that outruns sleep, in the affectionate glance that strengthens you during the day, in the face of forgiveness offered cheerfully when your insensitivity has been gross and relentless, it is the Lord you come to know. In marriage, as you experience such love, you come to know God Himself.

Finally, let the spouses themselves, made to the image of the living God and enjoying the authentic dignity of persons, be joined to one another in equal affection, harmony of mind, and the work of mutual sanctification. Thus they will follow Christ who is the principle *of life. Thus, too, by the joys and sacrifices of their vocation and through their faithful love, married people will become witnesses of the mystery of that love which the Lord revealed to the world by His dying and His rising up to life again.**

THE CHURCH'S ASSUMPTIONS

The Church's basic assumption, therefore, is faith in Jesus. This faith should be active; it should be within the worshiping community, and it should be growing in depth and maturity. We would be fooling ourselves if we thought that our Baptism automatically made us faith-full believers. Yet that is, unfortunately, our assumption. The grace of Baptism certainly opens our spirit to the grace of the Sacrament of Marriage, but it does not guarantee our cooperating with the grace present. If, therefore, neither you nor your fiancé(e) is willing to accept the responsibility and privilege of cooperating with the grace of the Sacrament, you should reexamine your intention of receiving the Sacrament in the Church.

Though you may think it unusual, it might be better to delay receiving the Sacrament if you have decided that the Lord, as He is experienced within the Church, is not for you. That would be the honest step to take, despite the pressures from home, from society, and from our culture. Only in making an honest response, one way or the other, can we be assured of God's blessing.

A second assumption of the Church is the indissolubility of marriage: a man and a woman promise to be for each other forever, just as Jesus promises to be for His bride, the Church, forever. To move toward this commitment you will need to gain a deeper knowledge of your fiancé(e) and yourself. Many parishes and dioceses sponsor "En-

* *The Documents of Vatican II,* Walter M. Abbott, S.J., ed. (New York: Association Press, 1966), p. 258.

gaged Encounter Weekends" which can help you in this. If possible, these weekends should be experienced well in advance of the wedding so that you and your fiancé(e) will have time together for sharing and reflection. If your parish priest does not mention such weekends, you should ask him, or call your diocesan Pre-Cana Office.

More than likely, your parish priest will help you. Listen to his advice; he usually has a wealth of experience in this area. Realistically, if engaged people are too young spiritually and/or psychologically for marriage, they will be unable to say "forever" with the correct attitude and will. The parish priest may be able to detect this; consider seriously his counsel.

No one, of course, can make a perfect commitment to Jesus; it is a growing response. Yet we need to be as prepared and informed as possible, so we can make the best response possible. In a true Christian marriage, this response will grow deeper and more mature as the years pass and each joy and hardship is faced and shared.

EXPECTATIONS

Assumptions should lead to expectations. If, for example, we assume the wood is dry, we can expect it to ignite when we light it. When the assumption is a reality, the expectation flowing from it will become a reality also. And so it is with marriage. If the Church's assumptions are real (or becoming real) in your life, you can expect certain results and experiences in your marriage relationship.

One of the first things to expect is the broadening of your individual spirituality. As a married person, you will have the opportunity to pray regularly with someone other than yourself who is now part of yourself. As a newly married couple, you should strive from the very onset of marriage to incorporate and actualize the power of the Lord, who calls you to be one in Him through a oneness together.

Shared experiences of prayer and worship, however, are only part of your expanded spirituality. Again and again you will seek the Lord for wisdom as you face life together. Opportunities to seek and to find, to trust and to hope, to forgive and be forgiven will abound. However, they are only that—opportunities. They will not be real for you until you choose them.

Marriage, therefore, will invite you, as a couple, to choose the Lord and His Gospel again and again—despite the risk, despite the pressure, despite the lack of understanding and support from our culture and society. This invitation, when taken, will give you new eyes. No longer will you be forced to believe what you see—violence, hate, and mistrust. With faith, you will be able to see what you believe, namely, that we are in the hands of a loving Father who shares His very life with us through Jesus in His Spirit.

As you grow in the Sacrament of Marriage, you will also be invited to experience freedom: in decision making, in communication, in sharing love and affection and forgiveness. It all hinges, however, on assumption number one —a faithful response to Jesus.

THE COUPLE'S SPIRITUAL PREPARATION

All this might seem "pie in the sky." After all, how many newly married couples pray together, make decisions by seeking Jesus, and live a "new life" in what seems to be at times an old and uncaring world? More than likely, not enough move in that direction; yet the fact remains: this is what is meant to be for you. Be assured that there will be excitement and joy as you strive to center your life on the one source of life—Jesus who is Life.

Your parish Pre-Cana program can be an opportunity for you to begin this quest. Most parishes and dioceses offer extended courses which will help you better understand the Sacrament of Marriage, as well as your relationship as a couple. Do not shortchange yourself in this area. If your parish priest does not mention such a program, ask him; it is for your benefit. Do not be hindered by the length of these programs–some may go seven weeks–since the time of preparation is short when compared to the "forever" you will be pledging to one another.

Another time or opportunity for spiritual growth will be encountered as you prepare your liturgy together. As you prayerfully read the Scripture selections below and discuss the tone and rhythm of your wedding ceremony, you will be drawn deeper into the living Word who is Jesus. A simple method for praying the Scriptures is offered on pages 66 ff. The Scripture texts for the marriage ceremony are found in Chapter 5.

Finally, your own individual reflection will be crucial. A renewed experience of the Sacrament of Reconciliation,† formerly called the Sacrament of Penance, and participation, as a couple if possible, in the Eucharist will also be helpful in joining you together.

Above all, do not forget prayer. Without it you will not have life to share. There are many good books which might help you continue or begin. Some of these are listed above on page 6.

† The Sacrament of Reconciliation is also called the Sacrament of Peace. A book which might help you renew yourself in this Sacrament is *Your Confession: Using the New Ritual* by Leonard Foley (Cincinnati: St. Anthony Messenger Press, 1975).

Two

INITIAL INTERVIEW

The initial interview of yourself and your fiancé(e) with the priest should be arranged approximately nine months to one year before the intended wedding date. At first glance this may seem like a long time ahead, but the time will be necessary if the priest and the couple are to raise and discuss the questions spoken of in the previous chapter. During this time, the priest will have an opportunity to understand your faith and spirituality. He will need insight into this aspect of your life if he is going to lead the prayer —your prayer—on the day of your wedding.

In order to make the most of this initial interview, it would be wise for you to call ahead and make an appointment. This will enable the priest to set aside a sufficient amount of time for you. Should you drop in unannounced, he may not be able to devote his full attention to you or may not be able to see you at all because of a previous appointment. A simple phone call will help to eliminate those possibilities, thereby making things easier for all concerned.

This first interview is meant to be a time of sharing—a time when priest and couple can begin to establish a trusting relationship. Expectations, responsibilities, and a sharing of ideas can take place during this encounter. Usually, the time and date of the wedding are set at this meeting; other details can be worked out in subsequent sessions.

Some questions that should be raised by the second meeting together include the following:

1. The parish's requirement for Pre-Cana preparation.
2. The question of dispensations for interfaith marriages should either partner be non-Catholic.
3. The Church offering (stipend), when it is due, and what it includes.

Should you have any questions after the initial interview, write them down so you will be able to bring them to your parish priest during this second interview. Should the priest fail to set up a second meeting and you have questions, do not hesitate to contact him.

During the time of these interviews, it would be helpful if you investigated any local guidelines that may be in effect. For example, some dioceses require a special program for youthful marriages, in which the couple participates in an in-depth interview and test by a trained professional counselor *before* a wedding date is set. Other parishes—because of Mass schedules or the shortages of priests—do not celebrate the Sacrament within the Mass. This is an unfortunate, though perhaps unavoidable, situation since the Sacrament of Marriage reveals its fullest meaning at the Eucharistic celebration.

While interviewing you, the priest will probably try to get to know you as a couple by asking questions about your families, your schooling, your financial situations, and your religious backgrounds and practices. The purpose of these questions is to help the priest assist you in preparing for the Sacrament. An honest and open dialogue is needed for the preparation time, if it is to be fulfilling. More than likely, the initial interview will be followed by one or two others. This would be in addition to the Pre-Cana instruction.

In some parishes, a deacon and/or laymen and women assist with these interviews. Should this be the case, be as open with them as you would with a priest. They too share in the ministry, and their time with you can be special for all concerned.

REQUIRED DOCUMENTS

During this time of preparation, several documents will be required to verify your freedom to marry in the Church. The first two are needed for a couple's protection lest either individual fail to acknowledge a previous religious or civil marriage.

1. Baptismal Certificate. The Church requires some proof of Baptism. Should you be a baptized Catholic, you will be asked to get a recent copy. This is done by writing or calling the place of Baptism and requesting a new copy. Since the back of the certificate notes any previous marriages, this recent copy would be an indication of your freedom to marry. When your marriage takes place, your parish priest will notify the officials at the place of Baptism. They, in turn, will enter the wedding date in the Baptismal Register. If you were adopted, rather than a natural, child, you may have to contact the Chancery Office in your diocese for a copy of the Baptism certificate.

A baptized non-Catholic must also present a Baptism certificate in order to obtain the dispensation for mixed religion (see page 18 for information on Interfaith Marriages.)

2. Letter of Freedom. This is a statement which testifies that you have never contracted marriage, either civilly or in a church service. The person you ask to write this statement should be someone who has known you for a substantial period of time. A parent, brother, or sister is the one usually asked.

3. Letter of Permission. This is a statement from parents testifying to the fact that they give their permission for the marriage of a son or daughter who is under twenty-one years of age.

4. Premarital Investigation. This is a simple data sheet listing the couple's names, family backgrounds, and religious attitudes. Though the term "investigation" sounds threatening, there is no real cause for anxiety. More than likely, the priest will gather the necessary information from you in an informal way, trying, as best as he can, to put you at ease. A great deal, of course, depends on the priest and how he manages the interview.

5. Publication of Banns. Usually the wedding takes place in the bride's parish. The groom, in that case, will need a letter of notification from his parish that his banns will be announced there three times; this notification is then turned over to the bride's parish. To obtain this notification, the groom should simply go to the rectory and arrangements will be made. If for some reason the wedding takes place in the groom's parish or any other parish, the bride will then need a similar letter of notification. In the latter case she may also be asked to receive from her pastor or parish priest a notification of freedom to marry outside her proper parish. The parish priest should be asked what the diocese requires.

INTERFAITH MARRIAGES

In the past, interfaith marriages (also called "mixed marriages") had been a source of pain and misunderstanding for those involved. It is probably within your parents' memory that interfaith marriages were frowned upon and agreed to with great reluctance. Perhaps, if they were of different faiths, your parents were married in the rectory or the vestibule of the church because they were not permitted to approach the altar. We should be thankful that this attitude has changed in today's Church. Receiving the necessary dispensations for an interfaith marriage is rather routine. This is not to assume, however, that a couple entering into an interfaith marriage should do so with routine preparation. In fact, an interfaith marriage requires a deeper questioning and reflecting on the part of both individuals.

In order for an interfaith marriage to take place with Church approval, several dispensations may be required, depending on the situation. Usually the process is quite simple. On *rare* occasions, these dispensations are not given. Should this be the case, it is probably because a complicating factor has arisen, such as the need for an annulment.

One or more of the following dispensations will probably affect you:

1. **Mixed Religion.** This is needed for the marriage between a baptized Catholic and a baptized non-Catholic.

2. **Disparity of Worship.** This is needed for the marriage between a baptized Catholic and an unbaptized partner.

3. **Dispensation from Form.** This is required if the couple is getting married in a non-Catholic ceremony. Such a dispensation is never given for the marriage of two Catholics.

It should be noted that a parish does not publish the banns of marriage for an interfaith marriage. Should you want them announced, make sure you mention this to the priest.

Should your non-Catholic fiancé(e) desire his/her minister or rabbi to assist at the wedding in the Catholic place of worship, it is permitted. Details should be worked out with the Catholic officiant well in advance of the ceremony.* Should you be getting married in a non-Catholic ceremony, a Catholic priest may be asked to assist. You should check with your priest to see if it is possible. If

* A minister or rabbi may be invited to read a Scripture passage, pray one of the prayers, give a blessing, and/or address appropriate words to the congregation. Proclaiming the Gospel and preaching the Word, however, is reserved for the priest or deacon.

the wedding is scheduled for a Sunday, he may not be available because of his Sunday Mass schedule. With the proper dispensations, however, the priest is not needed for the Sacrament to be recognized by the Catholic community.

In order to obtain dispensations for an interfaith marriage, it will be required that the Catholic individual signs a promise to do all that can be done to rear the children as Catholics. The full text, which must be signed or, under special circumstances verbally agreed to, reads:

> *"I reaffirm my faith in Jesus Christ and, with God's help, intend to continue living that faith in the Catholic Church. I promise to do all in my power to share the faith I have received with our children by having them baptized and reared as Catholics."*

Please note that the non-Catholic partner does not have to sign the promise. This is a promise that the Catholic partner must make. Failure to agree to this statement would probably result in a failure to obtain the dispensations.

Implicit in this promise is the assumption that the Catholic party in an interfaith marriage will continue to practice the faith with reverence and fidelity. Likewise, it is assumed that the non-Catholic will continue to seek the truth in whatever way he or she is led.

Recalling to mind the Church's basic assumption (page 11)—faith in Jesus—it is easy to understand why the Church challenges the Catholic partner with the above promise. Quite often, the couple in an interfaith marriage (and sometimes among baptized Catholics!) try to delay a decision in this area until a later date. This is usually done for the sake of "harmony." "Father," they will say, "we want our children to choose whatever religion they desire. Therefore, we don't want to force any particular religion on them until they can decide."

Such an attitude in a Catholic seems to show a lack of understanding. If, for example, belief in Jesus were really a part of an individual's experience, that person would not want a child brought up without the same opportunity to believe in Jesus. The joy and excitement that comes from knowing the Lord would be such that a Catholic would want his/her child to know the same.

For two baptized Catholics to hold the "decide later" view is totally untenable; such views could lead to questioning by the priest about their receiving the Sacrament of Marriage. In an interfaith marriage it is more understandable, since the non-Catholic partner may feel just as strongly as the Catholic partner regarding religious practice within a particular church community or ecclesial framework. This is why it is important for the interfaith couple to discuss openly and freely their positions before the marriage. Such a discussion is not intended to convince either partner that his or her belief is less than the other's. On the contrary, the purpose of this discussion is to discover the depth of your fiancé(e)'s faith, the traditions by which that faith is expressed, and the possible ways it may be shared with one another. This is especially helpful in a Jewish-Catholic marriage (or the marriage between a Catholic and an unbaptized person) where the liturgical and cultural expressions of your fiancé(e)'s faith are probably unfamiliar to you.

SECOND MARRIAGES

Oftentimes a couple seeks to be married in the Church though one or both partners had been married previously outside the Church. Can anything be done?

Unfortunately, a simple answer cannot be given. Each couple's situation is unique, and requires special attention. However, there are several "indicators" which might help you prepare for this part of the interview:

1. If the previously married partner is Catholic, and he/she had been married in a Church-approved ceremony—Catholic or non-Catholic—an annulment will be necessary.

The type of annulment required for this situation usually takes time to acquire. If one is needed, you should contact your parish priest well in advance of the intended wedding date.

2. If the previously married partner is a Catholic who had been married in a non-Catholic or civil ceremony without the Church's permission, i.e., without the necessary dispensations, a Decree of Nullity based on Defect of Canonical Form will be required. The process to obtain this annulment is rather routine in most dioceses and does not usually require as much time as the previous type.

If it is determined that an annulment is needed, do not be surprised when the priest does not set a date for the wedding. He is not permitted to do so until the annulment is processed. Your priest will help you make the necessary contacts to begin the process should it be necessary. Since each diocese has its own guidelines for granting annulments, it is important that you discover your diocese's policy as soon as you can.

If either or both partners is a widow or widower, it will be necessary to obtain the death certificate of the deceased spouse. This is needed to prove your freedom to marry since your Baptismal certificate would have noted that you had previously contracted marriage.

SUMMARY

All of these forms and dispensations may seem confusing or a waste of time. Try to remember, however, that the Church is concerned with maintaining her two basic assumptions (pages 11–12). Therefore, she will always strive to discover and resolve any situation where those assumptions may not be operative. The annulments, dispensations, etc., are all toward that end. Be assured that an honest and open dialogue with your priest during this time will help to make the process move more easily.

Three

THE LITURGICAL CELEBRATION

We now approach the most personal part of your marriage preparation: planning the liturgical celebration itself. It is in this area that you as a couple are invited to make a personal statement of faith and belief in the Lord and in each other. This, therefore, will require thought, prayer, and discussion with one another. You should plan on giving as much time and consideration to this as you would to any other details of your wedding day.

Above all, do not delegate the planning of the celebration to someone else, whether that someone be priest or friend. To do so would be to miss a perfect opportunity for you both to enter into the joy and excitement of this time of grace. The more you are personally involved in the arrangements, the more the celebration will be your own.

In order to help you through this unfamiliar territory, I have covered it in two separate chapters. This chapter gives an overview of the marriage ceremony, including a brief discussion of some available options which would enable you to add a personal touch to the ceremony. Chapter 4 will describe the Rite itself and lead you, step by step, through the ceremony. Each chapter contains several subdivisions that further suggest and explain different ways your wedding ceremony can be a memorable occasion for all.

MASS OR CEREMONY?

The first question to be raised about the liturgical portion of your wedding is whether or not you will celebrate it within the context of a Nuptial Mass. In making this decision, you may find it helpful to refer to the points made in the previous chapters: the wedding vows reveal their deepest meaning within the Eucharistic celebration because we also see and celebrate the wedding vow or covenant Jesus has made with us through His death on the cross.

Sometimes a couple comes into the rectory and requests "just the ceremony" since the Mass is "too long." Such a line of reasoning simply reveals a lack of understanding. In reality, the "extra time" it might take to recall the Lord's death and life in our midst should not be a factor in our decision. It's like saying to your spouse, "I can't kiss you this morning because I might be late for work." The time it takes is rather inconsequential to the meaning that is revealed.

Often, a couple will not choose a Nuptial Mass because their families are not "churchgoers." Should this be the case with you, remember that the wedding ceremony is *your* statement to the community on how you will be grace for the community. In such circumstances, you might even want to consider the printing of an inexpensive booklet which could help everyone–including the non-churchgoer–to join in the celebration. Some advice and suggestions on putting together such a booklet will be found on pages 158–75.

Perhaps you are hesitant about celebrating a Nuptial Mass because you or your wedding partner have not participated in the Eucharist for some time. Should this be the case, now is the time to begin anew! Your parish priest will help you receive the Sacrament of Reconciliation, if that is necessary, so that your celebration can be complete.

Should you and/or your wedding party intend to receive this Sacrament beforehand, it is advisable to make arrangements with the priest before the rehearsal night. It is not recommended that you receive the Sacrament of Reconciliation without giving yourself the correct amount of time needed for it to be a prayerful and reflective experience. Should you fail to notify the priest of your intentions, he may have other appointments which might prevent his giving you and your attendants the necessary time and attention. A simple phone call ahead of time would allow him to set aside sufficient time after the rehearsal or a few days before it.

Finally, it should be mentioned that a Nuptial Mass may also be celebrated for an interfaith marriage when certain circumstances are present: the non-Catholic party should be baptized and his/her Church or ecclesiastical community should have a belief in the Eucharist. Some couples prefer not to choose the Mass in this situation, however, since only the Catholic party and guests may receive Communion in a Catholic church. Others, however, choose the Mass anyway, as a sign of openness and unity within their different religious backgrounds. Check with your parish priest to see if there are any diocesan guidelines on the matter. Regardless of your decision, you as a couple should share your thoughts on this matter well before the wedding date itself.

THE TONE OR SPIRIT OF THE CELEBRATION

Having assisted many in their wedding preparations, I advise you to keep things simple. Nothing should detract from the movement and meaning of the service. All things —music, decorations, options, etc.—should point to and enhance the central meaning you desire to proclaim to each other and the community through your vows. Simplicity, therefore, should be the tone or spirit that is sought and conveyed. And so, in your planning, try to emphasize the sacred and religious dimensions of the moment. Nothing is wrong with the secular, but you must be aware of using the proper gesture in the proper place at the proper time.

Music

One way of assuring the correct tone for your ceremony is through the choice of music. At present, there are two differing views as to the type of music proper to a wedding ceremony. One holds that only sacred music, i.e., music written specifically for a religious function, is acceptable. The other holds that any song done tastefully can be a valid expression of the couple's intent during the ceremony. Both views hold some merit; neither can be dismissed without reflection.

In order to help you come to a good decision, I would like to offer some guidelines for your consideration.*

1. The musical judgment asks whether or not the music in question is good music *per se*. Is it expressive of the moment? Is it technically correct and aesthetically pleasing? Such a judgment is meant to eliminate music of poor quality or hackneyed expression. It removes the trite and the "cute" from the realm of choice. Granted, care must be taken that good musical judgment does not get confused with personal taste and preference. Competent musicians—familiar with music of several genres, including folk music—should be given a weighted voice in this matter.

2. The liturgical judgment asks whether or not the music, especially that with lyrics, is fitting for a place of worship. The words, images, and poetry should point the congregation's heart toward the love that God has for His people as it is manifested in the love and presence of the couple.

* These guidelines are adapted from the Archdiocese of Chicago Liturgy Training Program.

This facet of judgment must keep in mind that music is not a filler or something tacked on because there is a silent space. On the contrary, it is an element that should lead us to prayer and contribute to a spirit of worship. The liturgical judgment, therefore, should assure us that the music enhances the flow of worship and does not interrupt the sacred rite.

3. The pastoral judgment is the here-and-now decision about the music with your specific wedding in mind. This part of the judgment process looks at the factors that make your wedding unique: Is the congregation large or small, Catholic or non-Catholic, parishioners familiar with certain songs or visitors from various areas unfamiliar with the songs? The pastoral judgment, therefore, would decide whether or not the parts of the Mass would be sung, whether an Offertory soloist is called for, whether the people could sing a simple Communion refrain. To make such a judgment your parish priest and parish music coordinator/director should be consulted from the beginning stages of your preparation.

A traditional composition that does not fit into the wedding ceremony is the ever-popular "Ave Maria." Unless it is used somehow as an intercessory prayer to Mary for the couple, I do not see how its use can be justified.

4. The practical judgment deals with the parish's music capabilities. Remember that some parishes are limited in what they can do, and how well they can do it. Using music that cannot be played or sung properly or prayerfully will detract from your ceremony regardless of the composition's quality.

Prudent application of these guidelines will probably lead you to conclude that certain songs—though popular—are inappropriate for a wedding ceremony. Therefore, you should choose your music selections carefully. For the most part, couples choose songs that are lovely. However, more often than not, those songs simply do not say enough about the moment, nor do they point as directly as they should toward the mystery of Christ's action in us.

Folk Groups

When using a parish folk group, do not feel that the entire group must be in attendance. In cases such as this, less is really more. Therefore, ask several from the group rather than the entire ensemble. If there is a director of the group, that person should be contacted first, rather than your speaking to any one person.

Booklets

An inexpensive and useful way to help your guests participate in your wedding ceremony is printing a small booklet. Preparing your own booklet may take time, but the effort is well worth the relatively small price of having it printed. I caution against purchasing premade booklets on which your name is printed. Such booklets usually include all the options available, thereby making it difficult for your guests to know which to follow. It is better for you to choose the options and then have only your choices printed.

A booklet can be as simple or as complete as your guests require. If, for example, a Nuptial Mass is celebrated and many of your guests are unfamiliar with the Mass, it may be wise to print the parts of the Mass they would pray together. A sample booklet is provided in Appendix Two, pages 158–75.

An important part of any booklet is the printing of any necessary credits. Permission to print copyrighted material at weddings must be obtained from the publishers. It is usually granted free of charge for one time use. Should a fee be required, however, it is only just that you pay for the material used. Further details regarding copyrighted material and printed booklets are given in Appendix Two, pages 157–58.

While preparing the booklet, consult your parish priest and the church's music director so that you have the proper sections listed.

OPTIONS INVOLVING FAMILY AND/OR GUESTS

Entrance Rite

The traditional Entrance Rite has the family seated before the bride is escorted down the aisle by her father, a relative, or a friend. A variation of this would be to have both families met at the church entrance by the priest or deacon. A procession that would include ministers, acolytes, lectors, attendants, etc., priest or deacon, and the bride and groom accompanied by their parents would then proceed to the sanctuary. Such an entrance is a meaningful way to express the family's solidarity and joy during this celebration.

Scripture Readings

The Gospel, though chosen by the couple, is always proclaimed by the deacon or priest, though members of your wedding party, your families, or your guests may be invited to read the other Scripture texts. If you choose to do this, make sure that the reader is given a copy of the passage ahead of time. It is best if the lectionary is used during practice and during the wedding ceremony. Another idea, though not as acceptable, is to type the reading (double-spaced) on a single piece of paper and leave it on the lectern. This avoids the problem of digging into a pocket or handbag and reading from a crumpled piece of paper.

In addition, you might want your readers to practice

their selections in the church while using the amplifying system. This will prepare them to speak slowly and clearly so that the readings will be heard. The readers should remember to end each reading with the phrase, "The Word of the Lord," to which the people respond, "Thanks be to God."

General Intercessions

Often called the Prayer of the Faithful, this can be prepared and/or read by any member of the congregation. It is a beautiful way for someone such as the best man or maid of honor to pray for you and God's people. As with the reading of the Scriptures, a rehearsal is recommended.

This prayer should include petitions for the universal Church, the Church gathered for the ceremony, the families of the couple, and the couple themselves. Remember also the poor and the sick, as well as those who have died. For smoothness of delivery and response, end each petition with the phrase, "For this we pray to the Lord" or some similar invitation. A sample prayer is given on pages 43-44.

Presentation of the Gifts

Following the General Intercessions, the gifts of bread and wine are brought to the altar. Quite often, the parents of the bride and groom are chosen to present the gifts, but grandparents, brothers, and sisters can be included. If you choose this latter option, inform your parish priest and the parish music coordinator as to the number of people in the procession. This will enable the priest to expand the number of articles to be brought up, e.g., bread and wine, cruets, candles, incense, etc.; it also allows the music coordinator to select the proper composition for the procession.

Sign of Peace

This can be given in several ways. Usually the bride and groom exchange the Sign of Peace with those in the sanctuary. In addition they might also go to their parents and offer them the Sign of Peace. Do not hesitate to use a gesture which signifies love and affection such as an embrace or a kiss.

Sometimes the couple then proceeds throughout the church offering the Sign of Peace to their guests. Though well-intentioned, this prolongation of the Rite is really inappropriate, since it lengthens the Rite beyond its proper limits within the flow of the marriage ceremony. In addition, we must remember that the Sign of Peace does not originate with the bride or groom nor with the celebrant, but comes from the congregation gathered for celebration. Greetings and well-wishes, in this case, should be saved for the receiving line at the end of the ceremony.

Communion Under Both Species

The Rite of Marriage invites the bride and groom to receive Communion under both species, i.e., the bread and the wine. In addition, the entire wedding party and the congregation are permitted to receive in the same way. Ask your parish priest for the diocesan guidelines on this matter. He will be happy to advise you.

If Communion under both species is arranged for the entire congregation, you will need to have Special Ministers of the Eucharist to assist the priest or deacon. This extra effort will give your guests an opportunity for greater participation in the celebration.

OPTIONS THE COUPLE MAY CHOOSE

The following options are really local practices which are being used in some areas of the country but not others. They are not part of the Rite itself. In choosing such practices, the couple must remember that the Rite of Marriage has a liturgical rhythm and flow which should not be broken or cluttered with personal or dubious "pastoral" practices, of which there are many. The revised liturgy of Vatican II attempted to separate such practices from the celebration of the Sacraments. Caution, therefore, is needed should you attempt to add to the revised liturgy of the Rite of Marriage, lest elements be included which are repetitious or not in harmony with the liturgical prayer of the Church.

Vows

A couple must express their vows in the words of the Church. Should you desire to add other appropriate phrases, make sure that your additions do not alter or detract from the statement of commitment already expressed in the Ritual. Always keep the vows simple and clear. This is not the time for profound poetry or wordy promises.

Lighting of the Wedding Candle

A growing practice, used in several parts of the country, is the Lighting of the Wedding Candle. In this rite, a large candle is lit from two smaller candles held by the bride and groom. The meaning is obvious: the two now burn as one, joined together by the unifying grace of the Sacrament.

A variation of this practice would be for the parents of the couple to light the smaller candles and then present these to their children who in turn would light the main candle.

This ceremony could be used in one of three parts of the Marriage Rite: after the Blessing of the Rings, after the Nuptial Blessing, or after the reception of Communion. Sets of candles can be purchased in any religious-goods store, or you may use your own sets from home.

Prayer of the Couple

A couple may wish to offer their own prayer of petition or thanks. This is not to be confused with the wedding vow itself. If the prayer is a petition, it should be placed at the General Intercessions; if it is a prayer of thanksgiving, it might be placed after the Exchange of Rings. Because you will be nervous, it is best to write the prayer ahead of time, rather than to try a spontaneous or memorized one. Remember that the prayer should be heard by your guests, so a microphone may be required.

It is best for your prayer to be personal and from the heart. Should you be unsure of how to compose your own prayer, the following can be used verbatim or for guidance:

"Heavenly Father, you have called us to be one with you by being one with each other in marriage. Strengthen our resolve to grow in that oneness by a spirit of openness and forgiveness. Help our life together be the sign of your life and love within your people. Keep us always faithful to you and to each other. We ask this through Christ our Lord. Amen."

or

"Father Almighty, we praise you, and we thank you for joining us in this Sacrament. We know and be-

lieve that you have chosen us so that we might choose you through each other. We are filled with awe and excitement as we place ourselves this day forever at your service and the service of your people. We accept your plan for us as our plan for the marriage we will share together in you. All praise be yours, Almighty Father, forever and ever. Amen."

Visit to the Mary Shrine or Statue

A rather common request made by the bride (or by both bride and groom) is for an opportunity during a wedding ceremony to place a bouquet on the Blessed Virgin Mary's shrine or statue. Should you have a personal devotion to Our Lady, this might be a meaningful gesture.

You may be tempted to have the "Ave Maria" sung at this time, although the composition itself is far too long to accompany the action involved. Perhaps the organist might play a few bars of the piece and then bring the composition to a resolution after you have said a prayer at the shrine or statue. This visit is usually made before the recessional.

SUMMARY

The tone of your ceremony depends very much on the tone you set. Your choice of options, your instructions to the ushers, photographers, musicians, and other ministers will help shape and enhance your ceremony. Consult your priest. Remember to keep things simple: though many options are offered, not all need to be chosen. Avoid misdirecting the flow of the service because of the "extras" you desire. What worked well for one couple may not work for you if it does not spring from your faith and your heart.

Four

PREPARATION OF THE PLACE

The church or area where you celebrate your wedding is a sacred place. In order to highlight this reality, you should choose the type and style of decorations used for your wedding carefully. The flowers, banners,* vestments, candles, etc., are meant to help your guests celebrate with you on this joyous occasion. Therefore consider the placement of all things with care. In making plans to decorate the place of worship, be sure to consult with your parish priest to see if there are guidelines available for you.

All must be done to help draw your guests into the celebration. Time, patience, and planning are a far better investment than a huge outlay of money. A neatly printed booklet, for example, may give a fuller meaning to the celebration than white bows on each pew. Look always toward creating a total effect.

In preparing for your wedding, remember that music can be of great assistance. Gentle preludes and appropriate solos just before the actual ceremony help add that extra dimension that invites people to celebrate. Your parish's music coordinator will help you if you ask. Spend time planning with him or her.

At this point, I would like to mention wedding pictures. They're important because they "capture the moment"

* Two useful books on banner making are: Margot Carter Blair and Cathleen Ryan, *Banners and Flags: How to Sew a Celebration* (New York: Harcourt Brace Jovanovich, 1977), and Betty Wolfe, *The Banner Book* (Wilton, Conn.: Morehouse-Barlow Co., 1974).

when done well. To achieve this end, however, it is important that you instruct your photographer to avoid creating a distraction at the ceremony itself. Most photographers handle themselves at a wedding ceremony with sensitivity and professionalism. They truly capture the spirit of the day—the joy, the excitement, the beauty. Some, however, fail to appreciate the spirit you are trying to encourage and obtain. By creating a distracting atmosphere, they only "capture" what they have created, namely, distracted brides and grooms! Avoid this by speaking to the photographer ahead of time. Your guests will appreciate it if they are not disturbed during the ceremony, and you will appreciate it, years later, when you look again at the pictures from your wedding.

In this regard, it would be wise to check with your parish priest. It is not unusual for a parish to have certain guidelines which will help the photographer fulfill his responsibility.

Finally, in Chapter 6, page 129, you will find Checklist Three, which can be used when making the above preparations.

ENTRANCE RITE AND OPENING PRAYER

As mentioned on page 29, there are two options for the procession to the altar:

1. The traditional procession of the wedding party

or

2. The welcoming of the bride and groom and their families by the priest and his assistants at the door of the church, followed by a procession of all to the sanctuary.

Once the priest and the wedding party are in the sanctuary, the Opening Prayer is said. You have four from which to choose:†

† Letters can be used to indicate your choice in Checklist Five or Six, pages 133–37 and 145–48.

A. *Father,*
you have made the bond of marriage
a holy mystery,
a symbol of Christ's love for his Church.
Hear our prayers for N. and N.
With faith in you and in each other
they pledge their love today.
May their lives always bear witness
to the reality of that love.

We ask you this through our Lord Jesus Christ, your Son,
who lives and reigns with you and the Holy Spirit,
one God, for ever and ever. *106‡*

B. *Father,*
hear our prayers for N. and N.,
who today are united in marriage before your altar.
Give them your blessing,
and strengthen their love for each other.

We ask this through our Lord . . . *107*

C. *Almighty God,*
hear our prayers for N. and N.,
who have come here today
to be united in the sacrament of marriage.
Increase their faith in you and in each other,
and through them bless your Church (with Christian children)

We ask this through our Lord . . . *108*

D. *Father,*
when you created mankind
you willed that man and wife should be one.
Bind N. and N.

‡ Number is the one used in the Rite of Marriage.

in the loving union of marriage;
and make their love fruitful
so that they may be living witnesses
to your divine love in the world.

We ask this through our Lord . . . *109*

LITURGY OF THE WORD

The couple may choose one or two readings plus a Gospel passage. The first reading is usually followed by a Responsorial Psalm which is said or sung. A song may be appropriately substituted here. The Gospel may be preceded by an Alleluia Verse, which should always be sung if it is used. The guidelines on pages 26–27 can be consulted for further information.

The choices for the Liturgy of the Word are found in Chapter 5. Other Scripture passages may be chosen. It is not recommended that you choose non-scriptural readings.

RITE OF MARRIAGE

Before reviewing the Marriage Rite itself, you should be prepared to consider several possibilities. The exchange of vows (pages 40–41) can be in the form of a question put to you by the priest/deacon or a statement you make to each other. If the latter is chosen, you must decide on one of the following:

1. To memorize the words.
2. To read them from a book (perhaps held by the priest or deacon, acolyte, or attendant).
3. To repeat them after the priest or deacon.

The same choices hold true for the Exchange of Rings. No one way is better than the other. Regardless of the style chosen, however, it is important that your guests hear your exchange of vows. Remember, it is a community celebration of your promise to be for each other; it is not a private affair shared only by the bride and groom. A microphone, therefore, might be needed.

As mentioned on pages 32–34, several possible options are available after the Exchange of Rings, in the Candlelight Ceremony and/or the Prayer of the Couple. These are options and do not have to be chosen. Should you desire one or the other, try to incorporate it smoothly into the Rite. This would not be the time for a lengthy solo, vocal, or instrumental, lest the action and thrust of the Rite lose its momentum. If you choose music for this point, remember that the total movement of the ceremony needs to be considered.

What follows now is the Marriage Rite itself:

All stand, including the bride and bridegroom, and the priest addresses them in these or similar words:

My dear friends,* you have come together in this church so that the Lord may seal and strengthen your love in the presence of the Church's minister and this community. Christ abundantly blesses this love. He has already consecrated you in baptism and now he enriches and strengthens you by a special sacrament so that you may assume the duties of marriage in mutual and lasting fidelity. And so, in the presence of the Church, I ask you to state your intentions.†

* *At the discretion of the priest, other words which seem more suitable under the circumstances, such as friends or dearly beloved or brethren may be used. This also applies to parallel instances in the liturgy.*

† *In the marriage between a Catholic and an unbaptized person, the following introductory address is used:*

My dear friends, you have come together in this church so that the Lord may seal and strengthen your love in the presence of the Church's minister and this community. In this way you will be strengthened to keep mutual and lasting faith with each other and to carry out the other duties of marriage. And so, in the presence of the Church, I ask you to state your intentions.

The priest then questions them about their freedom of choice, faithfulness to each other, and the acceptance and upbringing of children:

N. and N., have you come here freely and without reservation to give yourselves to each other in marriage? Will you honor each other as man and wife for the rest of your lives?

The following question may be omitted if, for example, the couple is advanced in years:

Will you accept children lovingly from God, and bring them up according to the law of Christ and his Church?

Each answers the questions separately.

CONSENT: The priest invites the couple to declare their consent:

Since it is your intention to enter into marriage, join your right hands, and declare your consent before God and his Church.

They join hands.

The bridegroom says:

I, N., take you, N., to be my wife. I promise to be true to you in good times and in bad, in sickness and in health. I will love you and honor you all the days of my life.

The bride says:

I, N., take you, N., to be my husband. I promise to be true to you in good times and in bad, in sickness and in health. I will love you and honor you all the days of my life.

If, however, it seems preferable for pastoral reasons, the priest may obtain consent from the couple through questions.

First, he asks the bridegroom:

N., do you take N., to be your wife? Do you promise

to be true to her in good times and in bad, in sickness and in health, to love her and honor her all the days of your life?

The bridegroom: I do.

Then he asks the bride:

N., do you take N., to be your husband? Do you promise to be true to him in good times and in bad, in sickness and in health, to love him and honor him all the days of your life?

The bride: I do.

In the dioceses of the United States, the following form may also be used:

I, N., take you N., for my lawful wife, to have and to hold, from this day forward, for better, for worse, for richer, for poorer, in sickness and in health, until death do us part.

I, N., take you N., for my lawful husband, to have and to hold, from this day forward, for better, for worse, for richer, for poorer, in sickness and in health, until death do us part.

If it seems preferable for pastoral reasons for the priest to obtain consent from the couple through questions in the dioceses of the United States, the following alternative form may be used:

N., do you take N., for your lawful wife/husband, to have and to hold, from this day forward, for better, for worse, for richer, for poorer, in sickness and in health, until death do you part?

The bride/bridegroom: I do.

Receiving their consent, the priest says:

You have declared your consent before the Church. May the Lord in his goodness strengthen your consent and fill you both with his blessings. What God has joined, men must not divide.

Response: Amen.

BLESSING AND EXCHANGE OF RINGS

Priest:

A. May the Lord bless ✠ these rings
which you give to each other
as the sign of your love and fidelity. 27

R: Amen.

Other forms of the blessing of rings:

B. Lord, bless these rings which we bless ✠ in your name.
Grant that those who wear them
may always have a deep faith in each other.
May they do your will
and always live together
in peace, good will, and love.
We ask this through Christ our Lord. 110

R: Amen.

C. Lord,
bless ✠ and consecrate N. and N.
in their love for each other.
May these rings be a symbol
of true faith in each other,
and always remind them of their love.
Through Christ our Lord. 111

R: Amen.

The bridegroom places his wife's ring on her ring finger. He may say:

N., take this ring as a sign of my love and fidelity. In the name of the Father, and of the Son, and of the Holy Spirit.

The bride places her husband's ring on his ring finger. She may say:

N., take this ring as a sign of my love and fidelity. In the name of the Father, and of the Son, and of the Holy Spirit.

The General Intercessions (Prayer of the Faithful) follows.

GENERAL INTERCESSIONS

Technically, the General Intercessions, or Prayer of the Faithful, is part of the Marriage Rite. It is separated here so that several examples might be given.

Priest: *Heavenly Father, we gather here today to celebrate the marriage of N. and N. We know our brokenness and our needs, none of which can be healed without your love. And so, confident of your care and concern, we pray.*

Lector: We pray for your people, your Church. Let her always be a source of light and strength for the married couples in her midst. For this we pray to the Lord.

Response: LORD, HEAR OUR PRAYER.

Lector: We pray for your people joined in celebration this happy day. Strengthen our resolve to love you and each other with greater depth and sincerity. For this we pray to the Lord.

Response: LORD, HEAR OUR PRAYER.

Lector: We pray for N. and N. Unite them through the grace of your Holy Spirit so they may be channels of grace for one another and for your people. For this we pray to the Lord.

Response: LORD, HEAR OUR PRAYER.

Lector: We pray for those among us who are ill, especially those whose illness comes from the poverty that surrounds them. Grant them your healing strength by sending them believers who will minister to their physical needs. For this we pray to the Lord.

Response: LORD, HEAR OUR PRAYER.

Lector: We pray for those who have died, especially N. and N. Grant them peace in your kingdom. For this we pray to the Lord.

Response: LORD, HEAR OUR PRAYER.

Priest: *Loving Father, we place our lives in your hands, confident that you will always be our strength and protection. We ask this through Christ the Lord. Amen.*

Should the ceremony be taking place outside of Mass, the service is now drawn to a conclusion. After the last petition, but before the priest's concluding prayer, the Nuptial Blessing is given (pages 48–52). This is followed by the congregation's saying the Lord's Prayer. The ceremony then concludes with a Final Blessing (pages 54–56).

LITURGY OF THE EUCHARIST

The Lord Jesus instituted the memorial of His death and resurrection at the Last Supper. We continue to celebrate this reality when the Church community, led by the priest, carries out what the Lord did. The careful and prayerful planning of this section of your wedding Mass will help you participate more fully in this great memorial.

PRESENTATION OF THE GIFTS

For those couples celebrating their marriage at a Nuptial Mass, the service now continues with the presentation of the gifts. Many couples use this moment to incorporate members of their families into the service. Perhaps the grandparents might bring the gifts of bread and wine to the altar.

During this time, should music be chosen, the composition should speak to the action taking place, namely, the preparation of the banquet table before the Eucharistic Prayer takes place. It's best to choose a song everyone can join in singing, perhaps a simple refrain with a soloist singing the verses. A quiet instrumental piece would also be appropriate.

For this part of the liturgy, you are to choose one of the following prayers which the priest will say over the bread and wine.

A. *Lord,*
accept our offering
for this newly-married couple, N. and N.
By your love and providence you have brought them together;
now bless them all the days of their married life. *112*

B. *Lord,*
accept the gifts we offer you
on this happy day.
In your fatherly love
watch over and protect N. and N.,
whom you have united in marriage. *113*

C. *Lord,*
hear our prayers

and accept the gifts we offer for N. and N.
Today you have made them one in the sacrament of marriage.
May the mystery of Christ's unselfish love,
which we celebrate in this eucharist,
increase their love for you and for each other. 114

PREFACE

One of the following prayers, called the Preface, is used by the priest to begin the Eucharistic Prayer. Choose one.

A. *Father, all-powerful and ever-living God,*
we do well always and everywhere to give you thanks.

By this sacrament your grace unites man and woman
in an unbreakable bond of love and peace.

You have designed the chaste love of husband and wife
for the increase both of the human family
and of your own family born in baptism.

You are the loving Father of the world of nature;
you are the loving Father of the new creation of grace.

In Christian marriage you bring together the two orders of creation:
nature's gift of children enriches the world
and your grace enriches also your Church.

Through Christ the choirs of angels
and all the saints
praise and worship your glory.
May our voices blend with theirs
as we join in their unending hymn: 115

B. *Father, all-powerful and ever-living God,*

Joyce

LeFebvre

we do well always and everywhere to give you thanks
through Jesus Christ our Lord.

Through him you entered into a new covenant with your people.
You restored man to grace in the saving mystery of redemption.
You gave him a share in the divine life
through his union with Christ.
You made him an heir of Christ's eternal glory.

This outpouring of love in the new covenant of grace
is symbolized in the marriage covenant
that seals the love of husband and wife
and reflects your divine plan of love.

And so, with the angels and all the saints in heaven
we proclaim your glory
and join in their unending hymn of praise: 116

C. *Father, all-powerful and ever-living God,*
we do well always and everywhere to give you thanks.

You created man in love to share your divine life.
We see his high destiny in the love of husband and wife,
which bears the imprint of your own divine love.

Love is man's origin,
love is his constant calling,
love is his fulfillment in heaven.

The love of man and woman
is made holy in the sacrament of marriage,
and becomes the mirror of your everlasting love.

Through Christ the choirs of angels
and all the saints
praise and worship your glory.
May our voices blend with theirs
as we join in their unending hymn: 117

EUCHARISTIC PRAYER

After the Preface, the Eucharistic Prayer follows. You may choose one of the four said at Mass. If you choose Eucharistic Prayer IV, you should not choose one of the Prefaces just noted. That prayer has its own, special preface which must be used with the prayer.

MEMORIAL ACCLAMATION

There are four Memorial Acclamations. Choose one.

1. *Christ has died,*
   Christ is risen,
   Christ will come again.

2. *Dying you destroyed our death,*
   rising you restored our life.
   Lord Jesus, come in glory.

3. *When we eat this bread and drink this cup,*
   we proclaim your death, Lord Jesus,
   until you come in glory.

4. *Lord, by your cross and resurrection*
   you have set us free.
   You are the Savior of the world.

NUPTIAL BLESSING

After the Our Father, one of the following Nuptial Blessings is prayed over the married couple. Choose one.

A. *My dear friends, let us turn to the Lord and pray that he will bless with his grace this woman (or N.), now married in Christ to this man (or N.), and that (through the sacrament of the body and blood of Christ), he will unite in love the couple he has joined in this holy bond.*

Father, by your power you have made everything out of nothing.
In the beginning you created the universe
and made mankind in your own likeness.
You gave man the constant help of woman
so that man and woman should no longer be two, but one flesh,
and you teach us that what you have united
may never be divided.

Father, you have made the union of man and wife so holy a mystery
that it symbolizes the marriage of Christ and his Church.

Father, by your plan man and woman are united,
and married life has been established
as the one blessing that was not forfeited by original sin
or washed away in the flood.

Look with love upon this woman, your daughter,
now joined to her husabnd in marriage.
She asks your blessing.
Give her the grace of love and peace.
May she always follow the example of the holy women
whose praises are sung in the scriptures.

May her husband put his trust in her
and recognize that she is his equal
and the heir with him to the life of grace.
May he always honor her and love her
as Christ loves his bride, the Church.

Father, keep them always true to your commandments.
Keep them faithful in marriage
and let them be living examples of Christian life.

Give them the strength which comes from the gospel
so that they may be witnesses of Christ to others.
(Bless them with children
and help them to be good parents.
May they live to see their children's children.)
And, after a happy old age,
grant them fullness of life with the saints
in the kingdom of heaven. 33

B. Let us pray to the Lord for N. and N.
who come to God's altar at the beginning of their married life
so that they may always be united in love for each other
(as now they share in the body and blood of Christ.)

silent prayer

Holy Father, you created mankind in your own image
and made man and woman to be joined as husband and wife
in union of body and heart
and so fulfill their mission in this world.

Father, to reveal the plan of your love,
you made the union of husband and wife
an image of the covenant between you and your people.
In the fulfillment of this sacrament,
the marriage of Christian man and woman
is a sign of the marriage between Christ and the Church.
Father, stretch out your hand, and bless N. and N.

Lord, grant that as they begin to live this sacrament
they may share with each other the gifts of your love,
and become one in heart and mind
as witnesses to your presence in their marriage.
Help them to create a home together
(and give them children to be formed by the gospel
and to have a place in your family).

Give your blessings to N., your daughter,
so that she may be a good wife (and mother),
caring for the home,
faithful in love for her husband,
generous and kind.
Give your blessings to N., your son,
so that he may be a faithful husband
(and a good father).

Father, grant that as they come together to your table on earth,
so they may one day have the joy
of sharing your feast in heaven. 120

C. *My dear friends,*
let us ask God for his continued blessings
upon this bridegroom and his bride (or N. and N.).

silent prayer

Holy Father, creator of the universe,
maker of man and woman in your own likeness,
source of blessing for married life,
we humbly pray to you for this woman
who today is united with her husband in this sacrament of marriage.

May your fullest blessing come upon her and her husband

so that they may together rejoice in your gift of married love
(and enrich your Church with their children).

Lord, may they both praise you when they are happy
and turn to you in their sorrows.
May they be glad that you help them in their work
and know that you are with them in their need.
May they pray to you in the community of the Church,
and be your witnesses in the world.
May they reach old age in the company of their friends,
and come at last to the kingdom of heaven. *121*

Having completed the Nuptial Blessing, the priest now invites the congregation to exchange the Sign of Peace. Refer to page 31 for possible options available at this time.

At a Nuptial Mass, everyone is invited to receive Communion under both species, i.e., the bread and the wine. Receiving in this fashion is a beautiful sign for you and your guests. On pages 31–32 you will see some suggestions should you choose this option.

Remember, the Church teaches that the sacramental presence of the Lord is complete in either the bread or in the wine. When you receive the Host, you receive the Body and Blood of the Lord; when you receive from the cup, you receive the Body and Blood of the Lord.

After receiving Communion, couples sometimes choose to incorporate one of the following practices into the ceremony: Lighting of the Wedding Candle, the Prayer of the Couple, a visit to the Mary shrine or statue. Refer to pages 32–34 for further details.

PRAYER AFTER COMMUNION

Once Communion has been distributed, a prayer is said by the priest. Choose one.

A. *Lord,*
in your love
you have given us this eucharist
to unite us with one another and with you.
As you have made N. and N.
one in this sacrament of marriage
(and in the sharing of the one bread and the one cup),
so now make them one in love for each other.

We ask this through Christ our Lord. 122

B. *Lord,*
we who have shared the food of your table
pray for our friends N. and N.,
whom you have joined together in marriage.
Keep them close to you always.
May their love for each other
proclaim to all the world
their faith in you.

We ask this through Christ our Lord. 123

C. *Almighty God,*
may the sacrifice we have offered
and the eucharist we have shared
strengthen the love of N. and N.,
and give us all your fatherly aid.

We ask this through Christ our Lord. 124

FINAL BLESSING

The following may be used by the priest as a final blessing. Choose one.

A. *God the eternal Father keep you in love with each other,*
so that the peace of Christ may stay with you
and be always in your home.

R: Amen.

May (your children bless you),
your friends console you
and all men live in peace with you.

R: Amen.

May you always bear witness to the love of God in this world
so that the afflicted and the needy
will find in you generous friends,
and welcome you into the joys of heaven.

R: Amen.

And may almighty God bless you all,
the Father, and the Son, ✠ and the Holy Spirit.

R: Amen. *125*

B. *May God, the almighty Father,*
give you his joy
and bless you (in your children).

R: Amen.

May the only Son of God have mercy on you
and help you in good times and in bad.

R: Amen.

May the Holy Spirit of God
always fill your hearts with his love.

R: Amen.

And may almighty God bless you all,
the Father, and the Son, ✠ and the Holy Spirit.

R: Amen. *126*

C. *May the Lord Jesus, who was a guest at the wedding in Cana,*
bless you and your families and friends.

R: Amen.

May Jesus, who loved his Church to the end,
always fill your hearts with his love.

R: Amen.

May he grant that, as you believe in his resurrection,
so you may wait for him in joy and hope.

R: Amen.

And may almighty God bless you all,
the Father, and the Son, ✠ and the Holy Spirit.

R: Amen. *127*

D.‡ *May almighty God, with his Word of blessing, unite your hearts in the never-ending bond of pure love.*

R: Amen.

May your children bring you happiness, and may your generous love for them be returned to you, many times over.

R: Amen.

‡ An alternate final blessing that may be used in the dioceses of the United States.

May the peace of Christ live always in your hearts and in your home.
May you have true friends to stand by you, both in joy and in sorrow.
May you be ready and willing to help and comfort all who come to you in need.
And may the blessings promised to the compassionate be yours in abundance.

R: Amen.

May you find happiness and satisfaction in your work.
May daily problems never cause you undue anxiety, nor the desire for earthly possessions dominate your lives.
But may your hearts' first desire be always the good things waiting for you in the life of heaven.

R: Amen. *37*

May the Lord bless you with many happy years together, so that you may enjoy the rewards of a good life.
And after you have served him loyally in his kingdom on earth, may he welcome you to his eternal kingdom in heaven.

R: Amen. *37*

Five

INTRODUCTION

An important element in your wedding preparation will be your choosing appropriate Scripture passages for your wedding ceremony.* A couple may choose an Old Testament and/or a New Testament reading, in addition to the Gospel. The Responsorial Psalm is prayed after the first reading, while the Alleluia Verse, if used, is sung before the Gospel.

Anyone present at your wedding may read the Scriptures, with the exception of the Gospel, which is proclaimed by a deacon or priest. Chapter 3, page 29, offers some ideas for incorporating your guests in the presentation of the Word to the community. In addition to the readings listed below, any other Scripture passages from the lectionary may be chosen as alternatives.

Sometimes a couple would like a non-scriptural reading for their wedding. This is not possible since the Scriptures have an essential role in our being called to worship.

This chapter also includes reflections after each of the Scripture readings. These are offered to help you look more deeply into some of the questions and life situations that you may encounter before and after your marriage celebration.

---

* The Scripture selections that follow are from *The Jerusalem Bible*. Other translations are also acceptable when reading the Scriptures at your wedding ceremony. These include the *NAB, RSV, NRSV, NIV, TEL, NJBE.*

Please remember that the Scripture texts printed in this workbook are provided so you might choose from the many selections available. During the actual ceremony, however, one should read from the lectionary provided by your parish, not from *Your Catholic Wedding.*

OLD TESTAMENT READINGS

Old Testament–1

Genesis 1:26–28, 31a *OT–1*† *774–1*‡

God said, "Let us make man in our own image, in the likeness of ourselves, and let them be masters of the fish of the sea, the birds of heaven, the cattle, all the wild beasts and all the reptiles that crawl upon the earth."

God created man in the image of himself,
in the image of God he created him,
male and female he created them.

God blessed them, saying to them, "Be fruitful, multiply, fill the earth and conquer it. Be masters of the fish of the sea, the birds of heaven and all living animals on the earth." . . . God saw all he had made, and indeed it was very good.

The Word of the Lord.

REFLECTION: Continuing God's Creation

In marriage, God's free and spontaneous act of creation continues. Made in His image and likeness, we are called to move in His Spirit and with His Spirit; we are called to reflect through our creative faculties the beauty, the majesty, the power, and the love of God.

There will be so many ways where you as a couple, united by the grace of the Sacrament, will be able to take on this responsibility. Your lives together can now harness

† Use this reference number when filling out Checklist Five or Six, pages 133–37 and 145–48.

‡ This is the reference number for the reading as it is found in the lectionary.

the energy of two people filled with God's Spirit. As you relate to others, your creative powers can be manifested through words and gestures, through forgiveness and compassion, through love and joy. No longer are either of you alone in this endeavor: your spouse stands by your side to support, encourage, and affirm the creativity which is meant to spring from your heart. Just as God created in a word and a gesture, so you will be able to re-create through similar words and gestures.

In today's troubled world, your creativity–the creativity stemming from God Himself–is desperately needed. Couples willing to risk themselves so that the destructive elements of society can be overcome are very much needed. Men and women who are joined by love and are willing to gaze upon God's creation, accepting their responsibility toward that creation–that is who you can be, but only in Him. We will not be fully creative unless we are one with the Creator.

To be "masters of the fish of the sea, the birds of heaven, and all living animals on the earth" does not mean we destroy them. On the contrary, as believers we are called to imitate our Master, Jesus the Lord. As He tends and cares for us, helping our growth in every way, so we follow His creative example and carefully tend to "all living animals." We are told to conquer the earth; we are not told to destroy it. We conquer as Jesus conquers, through loving and careful service.

Since you are the image of God and since you have the grace of the Sacrament before you, move ahead with boldness, so that the Lord's creation can continue to be created through His love working in your marriage.

Old Testament—2

Genesis 2:18–24 *OT–2* *774–2*

Yahweh God said, "It is not good that the man should be alone. I will make him a helpmate." So from the soil Yahweh God fashioned all the wild beasts and all the birds of heaven. These he brought to the man to see what he would call them; each one was to bear the name the man would give it. The man gave names to all the cattle, all the birds of heaven and all the wild beasts. But no helpmate suitable for man was found for him. So Yahweh God made the man fall into a deep sleep. And while he slept, he took one of his ribs and enclosed it in flesh. Yahweh God built the rib he had taken from the man into a woman, and brought her to the man. The man exclaimed:

"This at last is bone from my bones,
and flesh from my flesh!
This is to be called woman,
for this was taken from man."

This is why a man leaves his father and mother and joins himself to his wife, and they become one body.

The Word of the Lord.

REFLECTION: Man and Woman—Co-workers in God's Plan

In this beautiful passage from Scripture, we hear God's plan for us unfold. Adam, the Man, was in need of a helpmate. The Lord, therefore, proceeds to provide beasts and birds for him to have; none is a suitable partner. And so God takes Adam's rib and forms from it the Woman, Eve, who is indeed a suitable helpmate.

A story of subordination or superiority? By no means. In fact, it is a story of equality between man and woman, for nothing else was suitable for Adam except that which came from his very flesh and nature. When the Scripture states that God took one of Adam's ribs, it is not to be concluded that the woman formed is less than the man. On the contrary, it is pointing out how she is the same as the man, she is from his side, i.e., part of him.

In addition to the equality expressed in this Scripture text, we must realize that Adam and Eve are meant to be more than mere companions for each other. Eve did not appear on the scene simply to fill up Adam's lonely days. Much more is implied in the text. Eve, the woman, is meant to be helpmate to Adam, the man. She is to rule with him, work with him, and generate with him the human family which was expected to continue God's human creation.

The Scripture, therefore, points out that Adam and Eve have a privileged job to perform together. If they fail to fulfill their responsibility, they will fail to complete one another. The helpmate is more than a friendly, interpersonally empathizing being who relates nicely to Adam. She is the co-creator with him of God's human family.

In their union, God in Jesus will paradoxically spring forth when the appointed time comes. In your married union, God will also emerge as you allow Him.

Old Testament—3

Genesis 24:48–51, 58–67 *OT–3* *774–3*

[The servant of Abraham said to Laban,] ". . . I blessed Yahweh, God of my master Abraham, who had so graciously led me to choose the daughter of my master's brother for his son. Now tell me whether you are prepared to show kindness and goodness to my master; if not, say so, and I shall know what to do."

Laban and Bethuel replied, "This is from Yahweh; it is not in our power to say yes or no to you. Rebekah is there before you. Take her and go; and let her become the wife of your master's son, as the Lord has decreed."

. . . They called Rebekah and asked her, "Do you want to leave with this man?" "I do," she replied. Accordingly they let their sister Rebekah go, with her nurse, and Abraham's servant and his men. They blessed Rebekah in these words:

> *"Sister of ours, increase*
> *to thousands and tens of thousands!*

May your descendants gain possession
of the gates of their enemies!"

Rebekah and her servants stood up, mounted the camels, and followed the man. The servant took Rebekah and departed.

Isaac, who lived in the Negeb, had meanwhile come into the wilderness of the well of Lahai Roi. Now Isaac went walking in the fields as evening fell, and looking up saw camels approaching. And Rebekah looked up and saw Isaac. She jumped down from her camel, and asked the servant, "Who is that man walking through the fields to meet us?" The servant replied, "That is my master"; then she took her veil and hid her face. The servant told Isaac the whole story, and Isaac led Rebekah into his tent and made her his wife; and he loved her. And so Isaac was consoled for the loss of his mother.

The Word of the Lord.

REFLECTION: Engaged Couples Encounter Weekend–Self-awareness as a Path to Oneness

It makes us a bit uncomfortable to read about prearranged marriages. Our sense of freedom is violated to think that a permanent love relationship can be set up by someone other than the people involved. During the time that this Old Testament passage was written, however, such was not the case. It was assumed that the union of a man and a woman would be arranged for them. After all, there were family ties to consider, treaties that needed collateral, dowries that had to be collected!

Strange to us, yes; but when you think of it, things are really not that different today. Surely our wedding was not "arranged," as the passage from Scripture describes, but are we all that free in deciding who will be our spouse?

True, it seems that your love for each other is sincere and without pretense. Everything looks "so right." Perhaps you even worked long and hard to finally convince your fiancé(e) that you were meant to be together. Yet is it not possible that these encounters with love are more "arranged" than we may care to imagine? For instance, look within yourself. List the *needs* you have that are crying out for fulfillment—needs your fiancé(e) seems to fulfill. Where do these needs come from? Are they healthy and in order? Are you in touch with them as part of you? Ask the same question of your fiancé(e). Get in touch with your deepest motivations and hold them up to the light. Are you marrying your fiancé(e) because he or she will get you out of an uncomfortable family setting? Are you pursuing your intended because you're bored with yourself? Are you lonely and find him or her company? Are you possessive and he or she wants to be possessed?

During your married life many unconscious needs will surface, change, and disappear. Current desires will give way to new ones. What draws you to your fiancé(e) now may change in a short time. It is for this reason that I believe today's marriages are, in a sense, still "arranged." Often, they are unconsciously "arranged" by the needs, desires, and hurts of the moment. We reach out now to fill a definite need now.

Such an arrangement, while acceptable during the initial stages of courtship must give way to something deeper. This occurs only as we grow in honest self-awareness. It will bear fruit only as we share that self-awareness with our fiancé(e).

An excellent program that will help you begin this process of discovery is the Engaged Couples Encounter Weekend. Ask your parish priest for details so that what might be an "arranged" marriage will become one that is truly chosen.

Old Testament—4

Tobit 7:9c–10, 11c–17 *OT–4* *774–4*

. . . Then Tobias said to Raphael, "Brother Azarias, will you ask Raguel to give me my sister Sarah?" Raguel overheard the words, and said to the young man, "Eat and drink, and make the most of your evening; no one else has the right to take my daughter Sarah—no one but you, my brother. In any case I, for my own part, am not at liberty to give her to anyone else, since you are her next of kin." . . . Tobias spoke out, "I will not hear of eating and drinking till you have come to a decision about me." Raguel answered, "Very well. Since, as prescribed by the Book of Moses, she is given to you, heaven itself decrees she shall be yours. I therefore entrust your sister to you. From now you are her brother and she is your sister. She is given to you from today and forever. The Lord of heaven favor you tonight, my child, and grant you his grace and peace." Raguel called for his daughter Sarah, took her by the hand and gave her to Tobias with these words, "I entrust her to you; the law and the ruling recorded in the Book of Moses assign her to you as your wife. Take her; take her home to your father's house with a good conscience. The God of heaven grant you a good journey in peace." Then he turned to her mother and asked her to fetch him writing paper. He drew up the marriage contract, how he gave his daughter as bride to Tobias according to the ordinance in the Law of Moses.

After this they began to eat and drink.

The Word of the Lord.

REFLECTION: Enjoying the Day

The wedding story of Tobias and Sarah does not seem to be much of a celebration. It was so businesslike, so brief, so formal. The external surrounding, however, did not detract from the deep love and desire Tobias had for Sarah.

And so with you. It will be easy to get distracted by the details and the practical aspects of marriage preparation. There *are* so many things which must be done: arrangements to be made, invitations to be sent, clothes to be readied. These, however, are externals; they are not the center of your wedding ceremony.

To be lost in the details, to be overly concerned that "it all works out" is a mind-set you should try to avoid. Your wedding preparation is meant to be a heartfelt celebration, a time of inner discovery and joy, a moment for family and friends to gather with joy and anticipation because you and your fiancé(e) have been joined together.

You might think at this point that such an approach is unrealistic or impractical. Yet you must strive to remain in focus lest your wedding ceremony get out of focus. No detail or arrangement is important or crucial enough to be worth a moment of anxiety or a sleepless night! Your friends and relatives will be more than pleased to know that you enjoyed your time of preparation because you kept things simple and care-free.

Enjoy your wedding day and the time which precedes it. Don't let the possibility of rain, or the cold coffee, or the wrong vegetable, or the missing flower ruin a day that is meant to be remembered with joy. Through it all, the details that precede your wedding should not destroy your heart's desire to rest secure in your spouse's love.

Old Testament—5

Tobit 8:4–9   OT–5   774–5

[Tobias said to Sarah,] "Get up, my sister! You and I must pray and petition our Lord to win his grace and his protection." She stood up, and they began praying for protection, and this was how he began:

"You are blessed, O God of our fathers;
blessed, too, is your name
for ever and ever.
Let the heavens bless you
and all things you have made
for evermore.

It was you who created Adam,
you who created Eve his wife

to be his help and support;
and from these two the human race was born.
It was you who said,
'It is not good that the man should be alone;
let us make him a helpmate like himself.'
And so I do not take my sister
for any lustful motive;
I do it in singleness of heart.
Be kind enough to have pity on her and on me
and bring us to old age together."

The Word of the Lord.

REFLECTION: Praying with Your Spouse

One of the most beautiful gifts you can offer to one another in the Sacrament of Marriage is the gift of prayer. Though you might, at first, experience some discomfort at the thought of praying together, the uneasiness should disappear as you try it.

As with any type of heartfelt sharing, prayer together can be a real source of strength for you. Do not be put off by your lack of experience or confidence. Begin in little ways: holding hands while you bless your food, Scripture sharing, or perhaps involvement in a small prayer group.

An obvious place for you to begin is, of course, the Eucharist, where your common celebration will be a binding power in your life. Do not stop there, however, lest you shortchange yourself with only part of the banquet prepared. In addition to the liturgical prayer of the Eucharist, you also need time for shared prayer, as well as private, individual prayer which could include petitions, thanksgiving, and praise.

What follows is a simple format that you and your fiancé(e) can use for shared prayer. It is quite easy and non-threatening, requiring nothing more than a bit of trust. Follow the steps listed, and see if you don't agree.

1. Begin with a short opening prayer. This can be a

spontaneous prayer or a standard one, such as "Come, Holy Spirit, fill the hearts of Your faithful, and kindle in them the fire of Your love. Send forth Your Spirit that we may be created and You shall renew the face of the earth."

2. Follow your opening prayer with a period of silence.

3. Choose a Scripture passage (the Psalms are especially good for this type of prayer) and slowly read it aloud. Have a time for silence after you read it aloud.

4. Now, reread the passage pausing after each thought or complete phrase. During the pauses, you and your fiancé(e) should feel an invitation to share aloud a prayer from your hearts in reference to the Scripture thought just read. This prayer might be in the form of a petition or a prayer of thanks, forgiveness, etc. Using the first few phrases from the prayer of Tobias and Sarah cited in this reading from Tobit, the prayer might go something like this:

First thought is read aloud:

"You are blessed, O God of our fathers; blessed, too, is your name for ever and ever."

Silence followed by shared prayer:

HUSBAND: Lord, I wish to thank You for incorporating me into Your family; for uniting me through Your Spirit with the saints of the past, and revealing Your love to me through Your saints here present.

WIFE: Lord, I wish to bless You and praise You for all You've given me today—the love of my husband, my time at work, the well-being of my family. Keep me always thankful for Your blessings.

Read aloud next thought phrase:

"Let the heavens bless you and all things you have made for evermore."

Silence followed by shared prayer:

WIFE: Father, I let so much pass by today. Where I should have rejoiced, I was silent, where I should have sought help, I complained. Grant me forgiveness.

HUSBAND: [*Perhaps silence. Remember, no one has to say something just for the sake of speaking!*]

5. End by praying aloud for one another and then saying the Lord's Prayer.

6. Silently embrace one another.

Old Testament—6

The Song of Songs 2:8–10, 14, 16a; 8:6–7
OT–6 774–6

THE BRIDE:

I hear my Beloved.
See how he comes
leaping on the mountains,
bounding over the hills.

My Beloved is like a gazelle,
like a young stag.

See where he stands
behind our wall.
He looks in at the window,
he peers through the lattice.

My Beloved lifts up his voice,
he says to me,
"Come then, my love,
my lovely one, come. . . .

My dove, hiding in the clefts of the rock,
in the coverts of the cliff,
show me your face,
let me hear your voice;
for your voice is sweet
and your face is beautiful." . . .

My Beloved is mine and I am his.

THE BRIDEGROOM:

Set me like a seal on your heart,
like a seal on your arm.
For love is strong as Death,
jealousy relentless as Sheol.
The flash of it is a flash of fire,
a flame of Yahweh himself.
Love no flood can quench,
no torrents drown.

The Word of the Lord.

REFLECTION: The Fire of Love

"For love is strong as Death." The phrase literally bounces from the page because we do not expect to hear the words "love" and "death" in the same breath. Yet, they are intimately and intricately bound.

Perhaps as young lovers, you do not consider death as part of your future. After all, it seems so far away, so distant. Why get morbid or anxious when you have your whole life together ahead of you? Your union together should not be overshadowed by an impending fear of death and separation.

Yet death of a kind in marriage is, in reality, a daily necessity. To ignore the final separation right now is understandable, but to ignore the place of "death" in your marriage is sheer folly. Without death in love, there is no love in life.

The death to which I refer is, of course, the daily times of "death" you will be called upon to bear. The death of an expected vacation because money is not available; the death of a salary increase because the promotion fell through; the death of a night's rest because of a sick child; the death of sexual fulfillment because your spouse is away; the death of "self-fulfillment" because you must care for the home. Yet, these deaths—more real and present than the final Death—are meant to be reservoirs of life, moments of grace, times for growth.

This kind of death, however, cannot bring about and strengthen love until it is accepted. To deny it, fight it, avoid it will only cause more pain and stunt growth in the process. To embrace it, as Jesus embraced His death, is to embrace victory and life.

There will be times, of course, when it seems so difficult, if not impossible. There will be times when it seems to be downright foolish. Yet, this is the way—not in a morbid, down-and-out sense—the way of victory as seen and experienced through our faith in Christ.

Enter into this "death" and you will enter into the flame of Love itself.

Old Testament—7

Ecclesiasticus 26:1–4, 13–16 *OT–7* *774–7*

Happy the husband of a really good wife;
the number of his days will be doubled.
A perfect wife is the joy of her husband,
he will live out the years of his life in peace.
A good wife is the best of portions,
reserved for those who fear the Lord;
rich or poor, they will be glad of heart,
cheerful of face, whatever the season. . . .

The grace of a wife will charm her husband,
her accomplishments will make him the stronger.
A silent wife is a gift from the Lord,
no price can be put on a well-trained character.
A modest wife is a boon twice over,
a chaste character cannot be weighed on scales.
Like the sun rising over the mountains of the Lord
is the beauty of a good wife in a well-kept house.

The Word of the Lord.

REFLECTION: One Hundred Percent or Nothing!

Although the description of the Old Testament's "perfect wife" might jar us a bit, the underlying truth remains. Whether husband or wife, we are called to offer ourselves as gift to the other, to care for and hold our spouse in a loving embrace.

During your courtship it would be helpful if you asked yourself some questions:

What areas of your life do you intend to offer your spouse?

What parts of your personality are you willing to change for your spouse's sake? How?

What part of your personality is going to be a difficulty in the relationship?

After thinking over your answers, speak lovingly and honestly to your fiancé(e). A "perfect" wife and a "perfect" husband do not pop from the sky already made. Yet you can come closer and closer to that reality as you look within and accept, as you reach out and change.

In such situations—which is to say in every situation—your responsibility is 100 percent. It is not fifty–fifty. It's all you and all him or her. Then it works. Of that, you can be certain, as certain as "the sun rising over the mountains of the Lord."

Old Testament—8

Jeremiah 31:31–32a, 33–34a *OT–8* *774–8*

See, the days are coming—it is Yahweh who speaks—when I will make a new covenant with the House of Israel (and the House of Judah), but not a covenant like the one I made with their ancestors on the day I took them by the hand to bring them out of the land of Egypt. . . . No, this is the covenant I will make with the House of

Israel when those days arrive–it is Yahweh who speaks. Deep within them I will plant my Law, writing it on their hearts. Then I will be their God and they shall be my people. There will be no further need for neighbor to try to teach neighbor, or brother to say to brother, "Learn to know Yahweh!" No, they will all know me, the least no less than the greatest . . .

The Word of the Lord.

REFLECTION: A Sign of Forever

Throughout the Old Testament, the sign of God's love for His people was the "covenant," or agreement, He made with them. This covenant was signified in several ways: during the time of Noah, a rainbow in the sky was the covenant sign; for Abraham, the fact that Sarah bore a child; for Moses, the Ten Commandments. Many people in the course of salvation history received these signs, which were meant to solidify and manifest physically the proper relationship to Him that God expected from His people.

Your marriage, like the Lord's relationship with His people, needs to be manifested by a sign. The sign itself will convey little power other than the power to "call to mind" the promise or relationship that it signifies. For you, a wedding ring may be that sign: small, lifeless, and possibly not expensive–yet in fact it is larger than life, full of power, and more valuable than the imagination can conceive.

During your married life, allow this sign to be proudly displayed. It is a constant reminder that you are for each other. As the ring has no ending point, so your life together should bring to fullness that reality–two are joined together forever.

More and more couples are using simple wedding bands for both the husband and wife. This makes a great deal of sense since *both* husband and wife pledge an eternal covenant with one another.

The passage from Jeremiah gives us a good point of reference in understanding this marriage covenant. Note that it is the Lord who is presenting Himself to His people. He is the one writing His Law on the hearts of His people. He is the one making the full effort, the result of which will be "they will all know me."

In your marriage, each has the privilege of giving all, of revealing yourself, and of planting your very spirit into the heart of the other, just as the Lord implants His Spirit into our hearts. There is no need to wait for a response from each other; the only need is to give, and to receive what is given in return. This is how God gives His Love to us.

Will there be times when this seems impossible? Yes. Will there be times when you cannot give any more? Yes. Will there be times when the world's opinion will lead you away from what it brands as an "insane" method of giving? Yes. Will those times ever negate the truth of the covenant? No.

RESPONSORIAL PSALMS

Responsorial Psalm—1

Psalm 33:12, 18, 20–21, 22 *RP–1** *776–1†*

REFRAIN: THE EARTH IS FULL OF THE GOODNESS OF THE LORD.

Happy the nation whose God is Yahweh,
the people he has chosen for his heritage.

But see how the eye of Yahweh is on those who fear him,
on those who rely on his love. . . .

* Use this reference number when filling out Checklist Five or Six, pages 133–37 and 145–48.

† This is the reference number for the psalm as found in the lectionary.

REFRAIN: THE EARTH IS FULL OF THE GOODNESS OF THE LORD.

Our soul awaits Yahweh,
he is our help and shield;
Our hearts rejoice in him,
we trust in his holy name.

REFRAIN: THE EARTH IS FULL OF THE GOODNESS OF THE LORD.

Yahweh, let your love rest on us
as our hope has rested in you.

REFRAIN: THE EARTH IS FULL OF THE GOODNESS OF THE LORD.

Responsorial Psalm—2

Psalm 34:2–3, 4–5, 6–7, 8–9 *RP–2* *776–2*

REFRAIN: I WILL BLESS THE LORD AT ALL TIMES.
Or: TASTE AND SEE THE GOODNESS OF THE LORD.

. . . my soul glories in Yahweh,
let the humble hear and rejoice.

Proclaim with me the greatness of Yahweh,
together let us extol his name.

REFRAIN: I WILL BLESS THE LORD AT ALL TIMES.
Or: TASTE AND SEE THE GOODNESS OF THE LORD.

I see Yahweh, and he answers me
and frees me from all my fears.

Every face turned to him grows brighter
and is never ashamed.

REFRAIN: I WILL BLESS THE LORD AT ALL TIMES.

Or: TASTE AND SEE THE GOODNESS OF THE LORD.

A cry goes up from the poor man, and Yahweh hears,
and helps him in all his troubles.

The angel of Yahweh pitches camp
around those who fear him; and he keeps them safe.

REFRAIN: I WILL BLESS THE LORD AT ALL TIMES.

Or: TASTE AND SEE THE GOODNESS OF THE LORD.

How good Yahweh is—only taste and see!
Happy the man who takes shelter in him.

Fear Yahweh, you his holy ones:
those who fear him want for nothing.

REFRAIN: I WILL BLESS THE LORD AT ALL TIMES.

Or: TASTE AND SEE THE GOODNESS OF THE LORD.

Responsorial Psalm—3

Psalm 103:1–2, 8 & 13, 17–18a *RP–3* *776–3*

REFRAIN: THE LORD IS KIND AND MERCIFUL.

Or: THE LORD'S KINDNESS IS EVERLASTING TO THOSE WHO FEAR HIM.

Bless Yahweh, my soul,
bless his holy name, all that is in me!
Bless Yahweh, my soul,
and remember all his kindnesses. . . .

REFRAIN: THE LORD IS KIND AND MERCIFUL.

Or: THE LORD'S KINDNESS IS EVERLASTING TO THOSE WHO FEAR HIM.

Yahweh is tender and compassionate,
slow to anger, most loving.

As tenderly as a father treats his children,
so Yahweh treats those who fear him . . .

REFRAIN: THE LORD IS KIND AND MERCIFUL.
Or: THE LORD'S KINDNESS IS EVERLASTING TO THOSE WHO FEAR HIM.

. . . yet Yahweh's love for those who fear him
lasts from all eternity and for ever,
like his goodness to their children's children,
as long as they keep his covenant . . .

REFRAIN: THE LORD IS KIND AND MERCIFUL.
Or: THE LORD'S KINDNESS IS EVERLASTING TO THOSE WHO FEAR HIM.

Responsorial Psalm—4

Psalm 112:1b,c–2, 3–4, 5–7a, 7b–8, 9
RP–4 776–4

REFRAIN: HAPPY ARE THOSE WHO DO WHAT THE LORD COMMANDS.
Or: ALLELUIA.

Happy the man who fears Yahweh
by joyfully keeping his commandments!

Children of such a man will be powers on earth,
descendants of the upright will always be blessed.

REFRAIN: HAPPY ARE THOSE WHO DO WHAT THE LORD COMMANDS.

Or: ALLELUIA.

There will be riches and wealth for his family
and his righteousness can never change.

For the upright he shines like a lamp in the dark,
he is merciful, tenderhearted, virtuous.

REFRAIN: HAPPY ARE THOSE WHO DO WHAT THE LORD COMMANDS.
Or: ALLELUIA.

Interest is not charged by this good man,
he is honest in all his dealings.

Kept safe by virtue, he is ever steadfast,
and leaves an imperishable memory behind him;

with constant heart, and confidence in Yahweh . . .

REFRAIN: HAPPY ARE THOSE WHO DO WHAT THE LORD COMMANDS.
Or: ALLELUIA.

. . . he need never fear bad news.
Steadfast in heart he overcomes his fears:
in the end he will triumph over his enemies.

REFRAIN: HAPPY ARE THOSE WHO DO WHAT THE LORD COMMANDS.
Or: ALLELUIA.

Quick to be generous, he gives to the poor,
his righteousness can never change,
men such as this will always be honored . . .

REFRAIN: HAPPY ARE THOSE WHO DO WHAT THE LORD COMMANDS.
Or: ALLELUIA.

Responsorial Psalm—5

Psalm 128:1–2, 3, 4–5a,c *RP–5* *776–5*

REFRAIN: HAPPY ARE THOSE WHO FEAR THE LORD.

Or: SEE HOW THE LORD BLESSES THOSE WHO FEAR HIM.

Happy, all those who fear Yahweh
and follow in his paths.

You will eat what your hands have worked for,
happiness and prosperity will be yours.

REFRAIN: HAPPY ARE THOSE WHO FEAR THE LORD.

Or: SEE HOW THE LORD BLESSES THOSE WHO FEAR HIM.

Your wife: a fruitful vine
on the inner walls of your house.
Your sons: around your table
like shoots around an olive tree.

REFRAIN: HAPPY ARE THOSE WHO FEAR THE LORD.

Or: SEE HOW THE LORD BLESSES THOSE WHO FEAR HIM.

Such are the blessings that fall
on the man who fears Yahweh.
May Yahweh bless you from Zion
all the days of your life!

REFRAIN: HAPPY ARE THOSE WHO FEAR THE LORD.

Or: SEE HOW THE LORD BLESSES THOSE WHO FEAR HIM.

Responsorial Psalm—6

Psalm 145:8–9, 10 & 15, 17–18 *RP–6* *776–6*

REFRAIN: THE LORD IS COMPASSIONATE TO ALL HIS CREATURES.

He, Yahweh, is merciful, tenderhearted,
slow to anger, very loving,

and universally kind; Yahweh's tenderness
embraces all his creatures.

REFRAIN: THE LORD IS COMPASSIONATE TO ALL HIS CREATURES.

Yahweh, all your creatures thank you,
and your faithful bless you.

Patiently all creatures look to you
to feed them throughout the year . . .

REFRAIN: THE LORD IS COMPASSIONATE TO ALL HIS CREATURES.

Righteous in all that he does,
Yahweh acts only out of love,
standing close to all who invoke him,
close to all who invoke Yahweh faithfully.

REFRAIN: THE LORD IS COMPASSIONATE TO ALL HIS CREATURES.

Responsorial Psalm—7

Psalm 148:1b–2, 3–4, 9–10, 11–12, 13–14a
RP–7 776–7

REFRAIN: LET ALL PRAISE THE NAME OF THE LORD.
Or: ALLELUIA.

Let heaven praise Yahweh:
praise him, heavenly heights,
praise him, all his angels,
praise him, all his armies!

REFRAIN: LET ALL PRAISE THE NAME OF THE LORD.
Or: ALLELUIA.

Praise him, sun and moon,
praise him, shining stars,
praise him, highest heavens,
and waters above the heavens!

REFRAIN: LET ALL PRAISE THE NAME OF THE LORD.
Or: ALLELUIA.

. . . mountains and hills,
orchards and forests,
wild animals and farm animals,
snakes and birds . . .

REFRAIN: LET ALL PRAISE THE NAME OF THE LORD.
Or: ALLELUIA.

. . . all kings on earth and nations,
princes, all rulers in the world,
young men and girls,
old people, and children too!

REFRAIN: LET ALL PRAISE THE NAME OF THE LORD.
Or: ALLELUIA.

Let them all praise the name of Yahweh,
for his name and no other is sublime,
transcending earth and heaven in majesty,
raising the fortunes of his people . . .

REFRAIN: LET ALL PRAISE THE NAME OF THE LORD.
Or: ALLELUIA.

NEW TESTAMENT READINGS

New Testament—1

Romans 8:31b–34, 35, 37–39 *NT–1*‡ *775–1**

With God on our side who can be against us? Since God did not spare his own Son, but gave him up to benefit us

‡ Use this reference number when filling out Checklist Five or Six, pages 133–37 and 145–48.
* This is the reference number for the reading as found in the lectionary.

all, we may be certain, after such a gift, that he will not refuse anything he can give. Could anyone accuse those that God has chosen? When God acquits, could anyone condemn? Could Christ Jesus? No! He not only died for us—he rose from the dead, and there at God's right hand he stands and pleads for us. . . .

Nothing therefore can come between us and the love of Christ, even if we are troubled or worried, or being persecuted, or lacking food or clothes, or being threatened or even attacked. . . . These are the trials through which we triumph, by the power of him who loved us.

For I am certain of this: neither death nor life, no angel, no prince, nothing that exists, nothing still to come, not any power, or height or depth, nor any created thing, can ever come between us and the love of God made visible in Christ Jesus our Lord.

The Word of the Lord.

REFLECTION: The Confidence of Faith

St. Paul's proclamation is a bold one: "Who can be against us?" He seems so confident, so sure. Yet, during your married life you will probably be able to name and identify many people and circumstances that seem to be against you. Was St. Paul all wrong—a dreamer who never let his feet touch the ground?

In this Scripture selection, we learn that faith does not remove difficulties from our life. They were certainly present to St. Paul. That is why he is able to compile such a lengthy list of trials and tribulations! In fact, our faith may momentarily highlight a difficulty so that, supported by grace, we may overcome it and be at peace. St. Paul sums it up beautifully when he says, "These are the trials through which we triumph, by the power of him who loved us."

No one can predict, of course, how these trials might enter our lives: a job may be terminated, a child be born with a serious disease, an ailing parent need constant attention, a spouse be bound by some addiction. Or, perhaps, the trial may be internal to your marriage: the temptation to judge, to be disloyal, to lack trust.

During these times, there will be some who try to convince you that the Lord is not there, that He does not care. Do not be deceived by them. At these times you need to believe, like Jesus, that you are in the arms of a loving Father. Remain constantly in Him and your faith will remain constant in the ups and downs of married life. After all, our God "did not spare his Son, but gave him up to benefit us all." His desire is to be God for us through every trial and tribulation, for "nothing can ever come between us and the love God made visible in Christ Jesus the Lord."

New Testament—2

Short version: Romans 12:1–2, 9–13
NT–2 775–2

Long version: Romans 12:1–2, 9–18

Verses 1–2

Think of God's mercy, my brothers, and worship him, I beg you, in a way that is worthy of thinking beings, by offering your living bodies as a holy sacrifice, truly pleasing to God. Do not model yourselves on the behavior of the world around you, but let your behavior change, modeled by your new mind. This is the only way to discover the will of God and know what is good, what it is that God wants, what is the perfect thing to do.

Verses 9–13

Do not let your love be a pretense, but sincerely prefer good to evil. Love each other as much as brothers should, and have a profound respect for each other. Work for the Lord with untiring effort and with earnestness of spirit. If you have hope, this will make you cheerful. Do not give up if trials come; and keep on praying. If any of the saints are in need you must share with them; and you should make hospitality your special care.

Verses 14–18

Bless those who persecute you; never curse them, bless them. Rejoice with those who rejoice and be sad with those in sorrow. Treat everyone with equal kindness; never be condescending but make real friends with the poor. Do not allow yourself to become self-satisfied. Never repay evil with evil but let everyone see that you are interested only in the highest ideals. Do all you can to live at peace with everyone.

The Word of the Lord.

REFLECTION: The Hospitality of the Heart

Your Sacrament of Marriage is not for you alone. All of God's people are meant to profit through the grace of your union. An important way for this to come about is by taking to heart St. Paul's exhortation on hospitality.

In a world and a society that keeps to itself, that plays its cards close to the chest, it is a sign of God's Spirit when you open your home and your heart in hospitality to others. By allowing your time and your possessions to be available for God's people, you provide a grace-full gesture of God's presence. How beautiful it is when Christian couples accept their guests–expected or unexpected–as a gift from God; how grace-full when you receive them as the gift they are, sent by the Father to draw you deeper into a life of Christian sharing.

If you desire to manifest this grace during your married life, begin by offering yourselves to each other so that you might be prepared for offering yourselves to others. To allow others the grace of being "at home" with you, you must begin by being "at home" with one another. Spend time together, structure into your day moments of sharing, walks on the beach or some secluded area, candlelight suppers, time when the phone is off the hook and the TV plug is out of the socket. Work at being "at home" with your spouse and the grace will be yours.

The hospitality of which St. Paul speaks will spring from your heart only as you grow in comfort and ease with each other. Should your time alone be tense or empty, your time of hospitality will be tense and empty. Seek, therefore, that peacefulness of heart which stems from your union with the Lord. In doing so, all who enter your home will be able to enter your heart.

New Testament—3

1 Corinthians 6:13c–15a, 17–20 *NT–3* *775–3*

[The] body—this is not meant for fornication; it is for the Lord, and the Lord for the body. God, who raised the Lord from the dead, will by his power raise us up too.

You know, surely, that your bodies are members making up the body of Christ. . . . But anyone who is joined to the Lord is one spirit with him.

Keep away from fornication. All the other sins are committed outside the body; but to fornicate is to sin against your own body. Your body, you know, is the temple of the Holy Spirit, who is in you since you received him from God. You are not your own property; you have been bought and paid for. That is why you should use your body for the glory of God.

The Word of the Lord.

REFLECTION: An Intimate Prayer

Not many couples choose this Scripture passage. They claim it emphasizes the Church's "hang-up with sex." Reflection on the truth of the Word, however, leads us to see a depth and a challenge well worth inspecting.

The passage clearly rejects acts of intimate lovemaking before the marriage vows of the couple are shared with the community. It may seem like an unreasonable command, especially in today's society where self-gratification is taken for granted. Yet, the Word of God is just that—

His Word—and we need to consider carefully its message.

The directive against premarital sex is not given because sexual relations are bad or evil. Quite the contrary. The gift of your self, which is offered to your partner during intercourse, is pure and beautiful. It is your prayer of union together before the Lord. Hence, the strong directive, since your prayer of union cannot be truly made until you proclaim that unity in the presence of the community. To "jump the gun," no matter how definite or close the wedding date, is to anticipate a promise of forever that, in fact, has not been made. Dates can be canceled, rings can be returned, promises to "be forever yours" can remain unspoken.

In addition, if you enter prematurely into this prayer of union, i.e., intercourse, the true center of your relationship remains clouded and hidden. During the time of courtship, you and your fiancé(e) should be moving toward genuine self-discovery. The elation, the closeness, and the emotions present during intercourse, however, really hamper any opportunity you have of uncovering your real needs and desires. They move you away from the center by seeming to *be* the center. The fact is, however, that the emotional and physical high of intercourse is not the center of your marriage, just as a leaf is not the center of the tree or a charismatic experience is not the center of your faith.

To share this experience before your marriage will lessen the opportunities you have of discovering your own inner reality and the inner reality of your fiancé(e). It is quite understandable why the desires are there: as your love grows and more time is spent together, you will naturally yearn to be in deeper union with your fiancé(e); the desire to hold, embrace, caress, kiss, and penetrate the very being of your intended spouse will automatically arise. To deny the existence of these desires is foolish; to let these desires dictate your actions is even more foolish.

During your time of courtship, do not think that your relationship is so deep and so secure that you will be able to ignore your feelings. You may think it is so, but realistically speaking, it is not. Try not to deceive yourself. Strive, rather, for self-discipline. Sometimes you will have to control those feelings and desires even during marriage (long business trips, times of pregnancy, etc.), so it is wise to learn now. Sharing honestly with one another your struggle with this directive is a good beginning.

Should your lives already be joined through intercourse, reconsider your decision to be united in this way at this time. Begin anew in the process of true self-discovery. Leave the old behind; the past is past. Free yourself from the confines of false growth structures and experiences, and reorganize your lifestyle so that true growth may occur.

New Testament—4

1 Corinthians 12:31–13:8a *NT–4* *775–4*

Be ambitious for the higher gifts. And I am going to show you a way that is better than any of them.

If I have all the eloquence of men or of angels, but speak without love, I am simply a gong booming or a cymbal clashing. If I have the gift of prophecy, understanding all the mysteries there are, and knowing everything, and if I have faith in all its fullness, to move mountains, but without love, then I am nothing at all. If I give away all that I possess, piece by piece, and if I even let them take my body to burn it, but am without love, it will do me no good whatever.

Love is always patient and kind; it is never jealous; love is never boastful or conceited; it is never rude or selfish; it does not take offense, and is not resentful. Love takes no pleasure in other people's sins but delights in the truth; it is always ready to excuse, to trust, to hope, and to endure whatever comes.

Love does not come to an end.

The Word of the Lord.

REFLECTION: Love Helps Growth

"How do I love thee? Let me count the ways." So the poet speaks to the beloved; so the engaged man and woman speak to each other. The word "love," however, conveys many levels of meaning that can easily distort the heart's intent. For example, do you "love" your partner the way you "love" a movie, or a sport, or work, or a hobby? Will you "love" and care for your spouse in the same way you "love" and care for your favorite outfit or car? It is amazing when given some thought, how a word used so frequently may not really convey the meaning desired.

Adding to the dilemma is the effect these various definitions have on your own lifestyle. After hearing and using the word "love" in many different contexts, it begins to lose its power. "Love" no longer becomes the word that is rooted in your heart's experience; it becomes a banner, a slogan, a catchphrase rather than an expression of intimate caring.

If you seriously consider the situation, you can break free. In the deepest part of your being, you sense a movement that is eternal and essential to your growth and fullness. You need to nurture that movement, that inner spirit, and allow it to be named. For generations it has been called "love," and you too can continue using the word. However, you must seek to defend that inner movement from contrary spirits and definitions; you must allow it to remain what it truly is, rather than compromise it because society misunderstands. This is why St. Paul's exhortation is so powerful: he points out that love never ends–it does not come and go, but remains and grows if it is true.

Growth, therefore, for you as individuals and as a couple is needed if you are to remain in love. This growth experience should be balanced, touching every facet of your persons–psychological as well as spiritual. For example, growth in self-awareness will enable you to look with perception on your actions and their effects on others. By seeking your true motivation, by your willingness to be vulnerable and defenseless, you will understand what St. Paul means when he says, "Love is . . . patient and kind . . . never jealous . . . boastful or conceited." By seeking spiritual growth through prayer, fasting, etc., you will be able to touch the Source of love as you gain strength from the Lord.

To seek a love relationship without seeking the necessary balance is to be satisfied with an illusion that is powerless and empty, an illusion that quotes the right words but cannot produce the reality. And so, be for your spouse the love that reveals reality through its patience, openness, and forgiveness. Strive to be for your spouse the love that never fails.

New Testament—5

Short version: Ephesians 5:2a, 25–32 NT–5 775–5

Long version: Ephesians 5:2a, 21–33

Verse 2a

[Follow] Christ by loving as he loved you, giving himself up in our place . . .

Verses 21–24

Give way to one another in obedience to Christ. Wives should regard their husbands as they regard the Lord, since as Christ is head of the Church and saves the whole body, so is a husband the head of his wife; and as the Church submits to Christ, so should wives to their husbands, in everything.

Verses 25–32

Husbands should love their wives just as Christ loved the Church and sacrificed himself for her to make her holy. He made her clean by washing her in water with a form of words, so that when he took her to himself she would be glorious, with no speck or wrinkle or anything like that, but holy and faultless. In the same way, husbands must love their wives as they love their own bodies; for a man to love his wife is for him to love himself. A man never hates his own body, but he feeds it and looks after it; and that is the way Christ treats the Church, because it is his body—and we are its living parts. For this reason a man must leave his father and mother and be joined to his wife, and the two will become one body. This mystery has many implications; but I am saying it applies to Christ and the Church.

Verse 33
To sum up; you too, each one of you, must love his wife as he loves himself; and let every wife respect her husband.

The Word of the Lord.

REFLECTION: Vulnerability in Love

Few couples—usually because of the female's objections—choose to use this passage. It is an unfortunate reaction since the passage is quite beautiful when understood in the proper context. However, we usually ignore or compromise or simply disregard the teaching presented here. After all, in this era of freedom and woman's rights, what wife wants to "submit" to her husband?

Putting emotions aside, however, you might be able to see the challenge offered here. To accept it is contrary to what today's society deems correct and acceptable; to ignore it, however, is contrary to the social order that our Lord may have in mind for your relationship with one another in the Body of Christ. What should you do?

As a point for reflection, I would like to suggest that the above conflict is really a question which bears upon your freedom to be vulnerable to God, your spouse, and your community. When you are vulnerable, you have nothing to protect you, you are defenseless and disarmed. To be invulnerable implies impregnability and hardness. Such qualities do not seem appropriate for a marriage relationship.

Genuine vulnerability requires risk taking based on your willingness to accept the other as well as yourself. This applies when you are vulnerable to God or to your spouse. Can you accept the other in the relationship or need you defend your rights? That is the question that must be answered.

When St. Paul states that the husband is "the head of his wife," he is pointing out to you the need for vulnerability. In his exhortation he is urging you to be disarmed, to defend nothing, to be free. His example is Jesus' own relationship with the Church, where Jesus, the head, is "disarming" in His love, thereby eliciting from His bride the proper response. This response is the Church's acceptance of Jesus' love by being submissive to that love.

Such a viewpoint is further clarified when St. Paul writes, "Husbands should love their wives just as Christ loved the Church and sacrificed himself for her . . ." Here the notion of true vulnerability is reinforced again in Jesus' death for love.

Do not, therefore, be confused. Reflection on the meaning of this Scripture text should not lead us to place one partner higher than the other; the reading does not claim one is better or more important. As a guideline for living, it simply gives you an indication of the way you are called to relate to one another in marriage.

Will you lose your freedom through this? No, not at all. In fact, your freedom will be fostered and enhanced, since both you and your spouse will now be free, through your vulnerability, to truly love one another.

New Testament—6

Colossians 3:12–17 *NT–6* *775–6*

You are God's chosen race, his saints; he loves you, and you should be clothed in sincere compassion, in kindness and humility, gentleness and patience. Bear with one another; forgive each other as soon as a quarrel begins. The Lord has forgiven you; now you must do the same. Over all these clothes, to keep them together and complete them, put on love. And may the peace of Christ reign in your hearts, because it is for this that you were called together as parts of one body. Always be thankful.

Let the message of Christ, in all its richness, find a home with you. Teach each other, and advise each other, in all wisdom. With gratitude in your hearts sing psalms and hymns and inspired songs to God; and never say or do anything except in the name of the Lord Jesus, giving thanks to God the Father through him.

The Word of the Lord.

REFLECTION: The Sacrament of Reconciliation—Choosing to Forgive

You each know what it means to be chosen: the joy of knowing you are special in the eyes of the beloved, the security you feel as your heart becomes the other's and the other's becomes yours. To be chosen means you are raised above, set apart, consecrated for a greater good. You and your future partner are that special person, for you have chosen each other and have begun the process of receiving the gift of the other into your life.

Yet, that specialness, the sense of being chosen, is a most fragile experience—especially in the early stages of marriage. Your trust and love, vibrant though not yet deep as all time, is easily uprooted, bent out of shape, shaken or crushed by simple words (or lack of them), feelings of deceptions and mistrust, as well as sundry pressures not yet experienced. Therefore, forgiveness will be necessary as the constant attitude of heart between you both.

Forgiveness, here, does not mean a simple "I'm sorry." That's only a beginning. Forgiveness means a righting of a wrong situation; a change of heart, thereby implying a change of action. Forgiveness implies immediacy. You "forgive each other as soon as a quarrel begins." The implication, of course, is that the quarrel never reaches its divisive finish since forgiveness takes place *as soon as it begins,* not after it is over.

Forgiveness requires openness and a willingness to put aside pride and hurt, to be attentive to small wounds lest they become festering sores; it implies a full-time approach to the other—a total immersion of self for the other. Jesus, of course, is the model. St. Paul puts it in this way: "The Lord has forgiven you; you must now do the same." His immersion into your life through His death on the cross grants you forgiveness. You are called to the same.

Implied in this experience is the reality that you have known yourselves as forgiven. To be forgiving, you should, therefore, receive forgiveness. For you as a married couple. the Sacrament of Reconciliation can be of great assistance in this endeavor. Although you may be uncomfortable with the experience, it may be wise to reconsider it as part of your growth process.†

The Church's experience in this Sacrament has grown and matured since you were in school. Therefore, speak to your parish priest. He will be anxious to help you. Learn how to receive forgiveness from the Lord so you may learn how to offer forgiveness to others.

New Testament—7

1 Peter 3:1–9 *NT–7* *775–7*

[Wives] should be obedient to their husbands. Then, if there are some husbands who have not yet obeyed the word, they may find themselves won over, without a word spoken, by the way their wives behave, when they see how faithful and conscientious they are. Do not dress up for show: doing up your hair, wearing gold bracelets and fine clothes; all this should be inside, in a person's heart, imperishable: the ornament of a sweet and gentle disposition —this is what is precious in the sight of God. That was how the holy women of the past dressed themselves attractively—they hoped in God and were tender and obedient to their husbands; like Sarah, who was obedient to Abraham, and called him her lord. You are now her chil-

† See footnote on page 14, above.

dren, as long as you live good lives and do not give way to fear or worry.

In the same way, husbands must treat their wives with consideration in their life together, respecting a woman as one who, though she may be the weaker partner, is equally an heir to the life of grace. This will stop anything from coming in the way of your prayers.

Finally: you should all agree among yourselves and be sympathetic; love the brothers, have compassion and be self-effacing. Never pay back one wrong with another, or an angry word with another one; instead, pay back with a blessing. That is what you are called to do, so that you inherit a blessing yourself.

The Word of the Lord.

REFLECTION: Obedience in Love

Obedience. Few people are comforted by the word. Weakness, submission, punishment seem to surround its meaning. In reality, however, the word can easily be set within the framework of love. In St. Paul's letter to the Philippians, he tells us, Jesus was obedient unto death. Here the word "obedient" means "gave ear to." He listened to His Father's desire and was obedient. He loved, and acted on that love.

In today's society, some people are claiming that this word "obedient" should be removed from the marriage readings. These critics see it as a threat to a woman's self-identity; they see it as an insult and a put-down. Such an interpretation really misses the point of the Scripture passage, while dismissing a beautiful exhortation for us all.

St. Peter's words here, as well as St. Paul's in Ephesians 5 (see pages 88–89), must first be seen in the context of a Christian community. During the Church's initial years, communities were structured according to the needs and talents of those involved. Within this structure, the husband and wife had a special and specific position. It is within this structure of community living that the word "obedient" must be understood. It is not a derogatory word, but one which allowed relationships in the Christian community to remain healthy and fruitful.

That, however, was yesterday. Should it carry the same force today? To answer that question you must first agree that the fullness of marriage reveals itself in the proper relationship between husband and wife *within the Christian community.* To be married and not part of the Christian community is to be without a full experience of the Sacrament. This lack is what the world takes for granted.

To get caught up with the notion that the scriptural relationship of man and woman is undesirable in today's world is to be influenced by a mentality which misses the point in the first place! St. Peter states quite clearly that the woman "is equally an heir to the life of grace." There is, then, no inequality—simply a difference of roles and gifts within the framework of Christ's Body.

As a concluding point for reflection, we might say—paraphrasing the English Christian writer and scholar C. S. Lewis—when love is lost in a marriage, it is, more than likely, where obedience has not been tried.

New Testament—8

1 John 3:18–24 *NT–8* *775–8*

My children,
our love is not to be just words or mere talk,
but something real and active;
only by this can we be certain
that we are children of the truth
and be able to quieten our conscience in his presence,
whatever accusations it may raise against us,
because God is greater than our conscience and he knows everything.
My dear people,
if we cannot be condemned by our own conscience,
we need not be afraid in God's presence,

and whatever we ask him,
we shall receive,
because we keep his commandments
and live the kind of life that he wants.
His commandments are these:
that we believe in the name of his Son Jesus Christ
and that we love one another
as he told us to.
Whoever keeps his commandments
lives in God and God lives in him.
We know that he lives in us
by the Spirit that he has given us.

The Word of the Lord.

REFLECTION: Live in the Light

Have you ever walked into a dark room, groping around, squinting, feeling, trying to identify shadows and shrouded objects, when suddenly, someone puts on the light? You're blinded; automatically your eyes close, your hand covering them, to shield them from the unexpected light. Until you adjust your vision, the light is quite annoying. In fact, it may appear that you managed better with the light off!

During your marriage, there will be many times when the light, i.e., the truth, seems too blinding to bear. The temptation would be to keep the light off; keep the truth bound; remain in the dark. Such an approach–though temporarily satisfying–does not give you a correct insight into Scripture living, nor does it remedy the problem. In fact, it may aggravate the situation beyond repair.

Sometimes you will rationalize the light away by convincing yourself that "it would only upset him/her" or "he/she would never trust me again." These seem to be useless speculations, none of which is founded on the depth of the love you profess to share with each other. How can love be love if it does not seek the light? How can love be love if it does not rest secure in the truth?

One of the most damaging experiences in your marriage would be to remain satisfied with the dark. Never get used to "squinting"; it may seem satisfying, but there's more to true sight than squinting. Your temptation will be to live in the dark "for the sake of peace" rather than to live in the light for the sake of love. It is not the only temptation you will experience, yet it is one which you need to fight at all costs.

New Testament—9

1 John 4:7–12 *NT–9* *775–9*

My dear people,
let us love one another
since love comes from God
and everyone who loves is begotten by God
and knows God.
Anyone who fails to love can never have known God,
because God is love.
God's love for us was revealed
when God sent into the world his only Son
so that we could have life through him;
this is the love I mean:
not our love for God,
but God's love for us when he sent his Son
to be the sacrifice that takes our sins away.
My dear people,
since God has loved us so much,
we too should love one another.
No one has ever seen God;
but as long as we love one another
God will live in us
and his love will be complete in us.

The Word of the Lord.

REFLECTION: Responsible Parenthood

To love as Jesus loves implies creation. Through His cross and resurrection, He who is the new Adam gave birth to a new creation: men and women empowered by His Spirit. You will continue that creation in the way you share your life and the way you care for the lives entrusted to you.

Responsible parenthood is an important part of that sharing. As mentioned throughout the pages of this book, marriage is not meant just for the couple's fulfillment. There is a communal dimension that cannot be overlooked. Part of that communal dimension is the family which you plan to nurture. Not to seek children in a marriage is, in Church tradition, a reason to declare the union null and void.

In today's society, where more and more couples are being influenced by all sides regarding the place of children in marriage, it will be to your advantage to discuss this topic with your fiancé(e). Perhaps you will decide to have a specific number of children in a certain number of years. Such a decision can be helpful since the time before the first child can then be used as an opportunity for growth in self-knowledge and awareness of your partner. Many couples claim from experience that the time between the ceremony and the first child is crucial: if it is too short, the couple feels hampered and cheated; if it is too long, the couple may find it difficult to readjust their lifestyle.

In planning your family, it is helpful to be aware of the Church's guidelines—they are there to assist you as you decide for the future. There is a great deal of information and misinformation available on this topic. To avoid discussing the matter would be to live in unreality. Seek to learn the Church's teaching in this area *and* the best way you can respond in conscience to that teaching.

A method which fits right into our country's "back-to-nature" movement is the Natural Family Planning method endorsed by Church leaders. This is different from the outdated calendar rhythm method which does not work for everyone. In fact, Natural Family Planning methods are as reliable as the Pill or sterilization. Using this method will help you postpone, plan, or avoid conception without using any unnatural methods.

To seek responsible parenthood in your marriage will foster communication and help you to use continence in a creative and loving way. Responsible parenthood relates to your total being, in a communal context, with a strong emphasis on your identity as a couple. For further information write or phone the organization below *before* your wedding date:

Couple-to-Couple League
PO Box 111184
Cincinnati, OH 45211
Telephone: 513-471-2000

New Testament—10

Revelation 19:1,5–9a *NT–10* *775–10*

[I, John,] seemed to hear the great sound of a huge crowd in heaven, singing, "Alleluia! Victory and glory and power to our God! . . ."

Then a voice came from the throne; it said, "Praise our God, you servants of his and all who, great or small, revere him." And I seemed to hear the voices of a huge crowd, like the sound of the ocean or the great roar of thunder, answering, "Alleluia! The reign of the Lord our God Almighty has begun; let us be glad and joyful and give praise to God, because this is the time for the marriage of the Lamb. His bride is ready, and she has been able to dress herself in dazzling white linen, because her linen is made of the good deeds of the saints." The angel said, "Write this: Happy are those who are invited to the wedding feast of the Lamb. . ."

The Word of the Lord.

REFLECTION: Worshiping as a Couple

The marriage celebration is meant to be a celebration: festive, joyful, colorful, memorable. To create such an environment, however, our attitude of faith is far more valuable than a wallet filled with money. Faith reminds us that our wedding is meant to echo the heavenly wedding of Jesus, the Lamb, with His bride, the Church.

A resounding echo it will be as you prepare for your nuptial: prayerfully reflecting on the readings, choosing the music and the decorations, continuing the celebration with an extended party for family and friends. It is all meant to work together toward one end—to celebrate the joyful announcement that two have become one!

The day of the celebration, however, is only the first part of the echo. Like all echoes, the celebration should repeat itself again and again—perhaps not as loudly or with as many people present, but certainly as clearly. It is during your Sunday worship together that you and your partner will echo over and over the astounding refrain, "Happy are those who are invited to the wedding feast of the Lamb."

For some couples, Sunday worship has become an intermittent affair dependent on time and circumstances. As a couple married in the Church, however, such an attitude needs to be reevaluated. After all, your model for marriage is Jesus Himself, who constantly rejoices in the Father's presence. As a married couple, you need to take your cue from Him—constantly rejoicing together in the Father's presence at Eucharist and in prayer.

There are times, as in interfaith marriages, when that "togetherness" seems to be stifled by Church law and discipline. As mentioned previously, however, such a barrier is not insurmountable. A sensitive spouse, aware of the differences, will be supportive in other ways. Perhaps shared prayer, family Scripture readings, or an occasional visit to the other's place of worship will help you remain together in the Father's presence.

In your marriage, the "reign of the Lord our God Almighty has begun" indeed. Support that reign with fervor and faith so you may always echo with joy the marriage celebration of the Lamb.

ALLELUIA VERSES

ALLELUIA VERSE–1 AV–1‡ 777–1*

1 John 4:8b, 11

God is love;
let us love one another as he has loved us.

ALLELUIA VERSE–2 AV–2 777–2

1 John 4:12

If we love one another
God will live in us in perfect love.

ALLELUIA VERSE–3 AV–3 777–3

1 John 4:16

He who lives in love, lives in God, and God in him.

ALLELUIA VERSE–4 AV–4 777–4

1 John 4:7b

Everyone who loves is born of God and knows him.

GOSPEL READINGS

Gospel–1

Matthew 5:1–12a *G–1‡* *778–1**

Seeing the crowds, [Jesus] went up the hill. There he

‡ Use this reference number when filling out Checklist Five or Six, pages 133–37 and 145–48.
* This is the reference number for the verse as found in the lectionary.

sat down and was joined by his disciples. Then he began to speak. This is what he taught them:

"How happy are the poor in spirit:
theirs is the kingdom of heaven.
Happy the gentle:
they shall have the earth for their heritage.
Happy those who mourn:
they shall be comforted.
Happy those who hunger and thirst for what is right:
they shall be satisfied.
Happy the merciful:
they shall have mercy shown them.
Happy the pure in heart:
they shall see God.
Happy the peacemakers:
they shall be called sons of God.
Happy those who are persecuted in the cause of right:
theirs is the kingdom of heaven.

"Happy are you when people abuse you and persecute you and speak all kinds of calumny against you on my account. Rejoice and be glad, for your reward will be great in heaven . . ."

The Gospel of the Lord.

REFLECTION: The Kingdom Within

I'm not the best skier in the world, but when I'm on the slopes, you can recognize that that's what I'm trying to do. I almost gave it up a couple of years ago because of a bad fall; the pain and the bruises forced me to think twice before resuming. But resume I did. About a year later, I spent a ten-day winter holiday on the ski slopes, but this time I played it smart. Rather than try it alone, I took lessons, spending the first day with a ski instructor—someone well versed in the art of skiing, someone who knew the trails, the ups and downs of the mountain.

I remember quite vividly our afternoon together. We were on one of the "more difficult" slopes. He told me what to do; I stared at him in disbelief. It seemed far too difficult, an impossible trail of twists and curves. And then, with a flourish, he simply said, "Follow me. Turn where I turn; jump where I jump." And so I did. Much to my amazement and delight, it worked. I succeeded, and enjoyed the run down the mountain. Where I had failed by myself, I succeeded with another.

And so with your Sacrament of Marriage. By following the Lord together you will be able to live and enjoy the Gospel norm presented in the Beatitudes of St. Matthew. Without assistance it seems so difficult, nearly impossible —an idealized goal that can never be reached. I thought that of the mountain slope marked "more difficult." Yet, by following my instructor, I succeeded. By following your instructor, Jesus, you too will succeed.

The "together" part of marriage is quite important here. The first place where you will have to practice and live the Beatitudes is in your own home. Together, try to live a life "poor in spirit"; together show mercy to one another; together be peacemakers for each other. The Kingdom of God dwells deep within. Seek that Kingdom within your spouse, and draw your spouse into your own heart so that he or she may find that Kingdom in you.

Gospel—2

Matthew 5:13–16 G–2 778–2

[Jesus said to his disciples:]

"You are the salt of the earth. But if salt becomes tasteless, what can make it salty again? It is good for nothing, and can only be thrown out to be trampled underfoot by men.

"You are the light of the world. A city built on a hilltop cannot be hidden. No one lights a lamp to put it under a tub; they put it on the lamp-stand where it shines for everyone in the house. In the same way your light must shine in the sight of men, so that, seeing your good works, they may give the praise to your Father in heaven."

The Gospel of the Lord.

REFLECTION: Spicing Up Your Marriage

While I was interviewing an engaged couple, the husband-to-be jokingly said to me, "I only ask that she use salt in the macaroni water. I can't stand my pasta unless it's boiled in salted water!" Being a priest of Italian background, it seemed like a reasonable request. But more than that, it brought to my attention just how important salt is for the flavoring of food.

So with your marriage. You will need to maintain an important "salt level" lest your relationship grow stale and tasteless, lest monotony and blandness overwhelm you.

What will be the "salt" of your marriage? What will you need to flavor the routine of daily living? Perhaps it will be a weekly movie, a candlelight dinner, or a time structured into your day when you can share your dreams. Every marriage has its own flavor pods which add a necessary dimension to married life. It is a simple, yet important, part of your marriage relationship, well worth discussing with your fiancé(e).

Perhaps the following questions will help you discover the type of "salt" you might use.

1. Is the silent love in your heart expressed by signs and gestures?

2. Are you able to celebrate the moment with your spouse although there's no "special occasion"?

3. Are you aware of important dates in your fiancé(e)'s life?

4. Are you verbal in expressing love and concern?

5. Do you express thanks for the gestures of love given to you?

Being conscious of these passing moments when some flavor might be added to your relationship will help you communicate the deeper reality of love that is present in your heart. Are these moments and gestures the essence of your relationship? Of course not. The essence is the love that binds you together. Is salt the essence of the macaroni dinner? No, but without the salt, the dinner doesn't seem quite as good. And so with your marriage. Those passing moments–innocuous in themselves–when "salt" can be added, will help flavor your relationship throughout the years ahead.

Gospel–3

Short version: Matthew 7:21, 24–25
G–3 *778–3*

Long version: Matthew 7:21, 24–29

Verse 21
[Jesus said to his disciples:]

"It is not those who say to me, 'Lord, Lord' who will enter the kingdom of heaven, but the person who does the will of my Father in heaven. . . ."

Verses 24–25
"Therefore, everyone who listens to these words of mine and acts on them will be like a sensible man who built his house on rock. Rain came down, floods rose, gales blew and hurled themselves against that house, and it did not fall: it was founded on rock. . . ."

Verses 26–29
"But everyone who listens to these words of mine and does not act on them will be like a stupid man who built his house on sand. Rain came down, floods rose, gales blew and struck that house and it fell; and what a fall it had!"

Jesus had now finished what he wanted to say, and his teaching made a deep impression on the people because he taught them with authority, and not like their own scribes.

The Gospel of the Lord.

REFLECTION: Investing in the Rock

Planning for the future is a wise investment of time. As a newly married couple, you will share dreams together over the span of your married life. These dreams will become a reality only as you plan and pace yourself—anticipating the future, yet not remaining so rigid that change is impossible.

Many young couples are able to begin their married life with the comforts and conveniences that are taken for granted in our society: a car, a TV, a dishwasher, etc. Similar comforts—signs of security—may have been acquired by your parents after several years of frugal living and careful saving. Yet, here they are right at your fingertips.

For the believer, building a house on rock has little to do with the securities or comforts our American culture takes for granted. As a young couple, therefore, your dream should transcend the second car, the private home, the high-salaried position. These are good, yet they are not the stuff which will keep you together.

During the time of courtship, it will be worthwhile to share your dreams with each other. Should you discover that they center on material possessions, you may want to reevaluate your focus of attention. Basing your heart's security on a materially prosperous marriage will only lead to frustration, disappointment, and broken dreams.

In addition, it would be wise to map out the path you might have to follow to fulfill your dreams of security. Will it require your being separated for long periods of time? Will it mean late hours and no relaxation? Will it put you in positions where your Christian faith cannot be nurtured? These are important questions for you to consider in discovering which "rock" you are using for your foundations.

The rocks our society seems to imply are strong foundation stones—wealth, social position, power, material possessions—are really the sands which will cave in on the unsuspecting couple who build their marriage on such foundations. Do not be deceived. There is only one Rock: the Lord; there is only one dream worth striving for: to live in His Kingdom *now* and forever.

Gospel—4

Matthew 19:3–6 *G–4* *778–4*

Some Pharisees approached him, and to test him they said, "Is it against the Law for a man to divorce his wife on any pretext whatever?" He answered, "Have you not read that the Creator from the beginning made them male and female and that he said: This is why a man must leave father and mother, and cling to his wife, and the two become one body? They are no longer two, therefore, but one body. So then, what God has united, man must not divide."

The Gospel of the Lord.

REFLECTION: Marriage Encounter—Tool for Communication

Rooted in the Church's tradition is the teaching on the permanence of the Marriage Sacrament. You, of course, are not thinking negatively about this since you've just started living your life together! It would not be a marriage in good faith if you were already worrying about a possible separation. Yet the fact remains that more and more couples find themselves in the throes of divorce and separation. It is a fact that must be dealt with, lest your marriage become part of the statistics. Simply to ignore the data at hand by saying, "Not us," shows fear and immaturity rather than deep and reflective love.

When studying the available data, we see that the divorce rate is very much founded on a "lack of love" between the couples. This catchphrase is vague enough to cover a multitude of experiences. However, whatever it means, it does not occur overnight: you do not love one day and not love the next. Love is far too complex and embracing for that.

What, then, are the signs that might indicate this "lack of love?" What are the clues that were missed before the end came? Many would claim that a lack of communication is a key. "I didn't realize he/she was like that" or "He/she's not the same as he/she was when we first met" are the refrains, repeated over and over. To combat this danger, therefore, you must practice speaking honestly from your heart; leave nothing to a guess or an assumption. Discipline yourself so that sharing your heart becomes easy and natural. Some couples have found that the technique used by Marriage Encounter couples is helpful in this area of communication. Ask your parish priest for information about this. If he does not know, write or phone the organization below:

Worldwide Marriage Encounter
PO Box 329
Felton, CA 95018
Telephone: 1-800-795-LOVE

False expectations are another possible area for concern. He/she wants to live simply, he/she wants the comforts of society; he/she wants four children, he/she wants none; he/she thought the other liked Mother, he/she thinks that Mother-in-law is a nuisance . . . on and on the differences multiply. To be united together in marriage, yet cling to unchanging or false expectations, will lead to an eventual crisis. Once again, communication is the key.

Money matters can also become a wedge in a marriage's permanence. How money is saved or spent all add or detract from the couple's stability. Again, communication is essential *before* the marriage, not only after it. Do not think that a practical approach in this area eliminates true love. In reality, it can strengthen it.

For a final point of reflection, you might say that God, through His Word, created you to be one in marriage, while you, through your silence, often destroy what God has created. The Father, speaking from His heart, gave you Jesus, the Word made flesh; you must follow the same example, always speaking from your heart to the person who has been united to you.

Gospel–5

Matthew 22:35–40 *G–5* *778–5*

[One of the Pharisees,] to disconcert him . . . put a question, "Master, which is the greatest commandment of the Law?" Jesus said, "You must love the Lord your God with all your heart, with all your soul, and with all your mind. This is the greatest and the first commandment. The second resembles it: You must love your neighbor as yourself. On these two commandments hang the whole Law, and the Prophets also."

The Gospel of the Lord.

REFLECTION: The Undiscovered Treasure

The love you offer your spouse is indeed a gift—a treasure only you can give. Yet should you believe your love is nothing because you are nothing, you won't be that anxious to give or secure in giving your gift freely and fully.

Love of God and love of neighbor are very much connected to love of self. There is no easily identified division among them. They seem to flow back and forth. This is why spiritual growth in marriage rests on our assisting one another to develop a healthy and wholesome self-love.

This self-love is quite different from the egocentricity that focuses all attention inward. Self-love in this context is more the type of love Jesus had for Himself—an ever-increasing awareness of His relationship with the Father, coupled to a deepened understanding that He was Son, Child of the Father. His acceptance of that reality tied it all together.

and trust and security. They sum up the dream of every married couple: to remain in love. All the signs are now pointing to that direction. There are deep feelings, shared experiences, and plans for the future; there are times of affection, forgiveness, and a great deal of laughter. You've got it made.

Remaining in love, however, goes beyond today; it's tomorrow as well. You must live today fully alive in each other, but tomorrow should be different since your capacity to love has been expanded by today's giving and receiving. It requires a willingness on your part to expand your capacity for loving by growing deeper.

There are several "rules" which may help you accomplish this. You've heard them all before, but the exhortation to "love one another" can never be overplayed. In reality, it is meant to be the song your heart sings again and again.

Openness. To be expanded by your spouse demands a willingness to crack open your shell, to let the seams split, to become other. I think of an acorn. If the shell does not split open, the acorn would not become the oak tree. In the openness, the acorn changes. By your openness you too will change as you become what you are meant to be.

Dialogue. This is the essential two-way conversation in marriage where heart listens to heart. This conversation is not limited to words, but includes other methods of communication: the affirmation of a loving glance, the affection of a gentle touch. As in all things worthwhile, dialogue must be worked at. You make it happen by beginning with trust and persevering in hope.

Vulnerability. Being defenseless in the presence of your spouse requires a real poverty. It implies that you have nothing to defend or cling to but the love you bear your spouse. Being vulnerable in this way opens you to pains and hurts and woundedness for the other and by the other. It also opens you to healing.

Thinking the Best. By thinking the best of your spouse in every situation, you are on the road to remaining in the love of the other. This does not mean that facts and feelings are denied; it does mean, however, that you avoid hasty conclusions, holding grudges, and refusing to listen with your heart.

Gospel—9

John 15:12–16 *G–9* *778–9*

[Jesus said to his disciples:]
"This is my commandment:
love one another,
as I have loved you.
A man can have no greater love
than to lay down his life for his friends.
You are my friends,
if you do what I command you.
I shall not call you servants any more,
because a servant does not know
his master's business;
I call you friends,
because I have made known to you
everything I have learned from my Father.
You did not choose me,
no, I chose you;
and I commissioned you
to go out and to bear fruit,
fruit that will last;
and then the Father will give you
anything you ask him in my name."

The Gospel of the Lord.

REFLECTION: Conditions Must Be Unconditional

"If you really loved me, you would . . ."—a deceptively

simple phrase which you will undoubtedly find yourself thinking or saying sometime during your marriage together. It is a phrase that cries out for a response; it moans for a hearing and an answer; it plays on all the levels of feelings—guilt, love, doubt—that are swirling inside each of us. It is also one of the most dangerous phrases and weapons in our marriage arsenal.

To live as one requires mutual trust and caring that transcends any conditional clause or statement beginning with "If you . . ." Using such a tool in your life together will seldom build the relationship into that citadel of love and union where the Spirit dwells in peace. The "if you . . ." phrase implies manipulation, lack of trust, and a tendency toward selfishness.

Compare this with a similar phrase from Jesus, "This is my commandment: love one another as I have loved you." Notice the difference. Jesus did not say, *if* you expect my love, love one another. His love was not contingent on the response. His love was free, unconditional, unilateral.

During your marriage there will be times when each of you will be called to love as Jesus does. No "ifs" will be involved; no bribes or conditions will be set. A simple, full-bodied, full-hearted offering will be expected. To add the conditional "if" to the response will eliminate the grace of the response.

Right now you may teasingly "bribe" one another with conditional phrases such as "If you really loved me, you wouldn't go . . ." or "Try to love me now the way I ask" or "If you really loved me you would not have forgotten to . . ." At the moment they may seem to be valid tests of real love. In future moments, however, they may become the barriers of true love.

Should your fiancé(e) be "failing" in his/her relationship with you now, a conditional clause that plays on guilt feelings will not solve the problem. Now is the time to look at your own expectations: Are they freely being met or do you have to beg for their fulfillment? Now is the time to read the barometer correctly so you can foresee what is to come.

Gospel—10

Short version: John 17:20–23 *G–10* *778–10*

Long version: John 17:20–26

Verses 20–23

[Jesus raised his eyes to heaven and prayed, saying:]

"I pray not only for these,
but for those also
who through their words will believe in me.
May they all be one.
Father, may they be one in us,
as you are in me and I am in you,
so that the world may believe it was you who sent me.
I have given them the glory you gave to me,
that they may be one as we are one.
With me in them and you in me,
may they be so completely one
that the world will realize that it was you who sent me
and that I have loved them as much as you loved me."

Verses 24–26

"Father,
I want those you have given me
to be with me where I am,
so that they may always see the glory
you have given me
because you loved me
before the foundation of the world.
Father, Righteous One,
the world has not known you,
but I have known you,
and these have known
that you have sent me.

I have made your name known to them
and will continue to make it known,
so that the love with which you loved me may be in them,
and so that I may be in them."

The Gospel of the Lord.

REFLECTION: Oneness in an Interfaith Marriage

Interfaith marriages were once feared by all Christian parents. The thought that their child might marry someone not from their faith was frightening. As a result, families often suffered irreparable damage because a "mixed marriage" was forbidden or unacceptable.

Happily, the situation today has changed substantially, if not dramatically. The Church's guidelines now allow an interfaith couple to experience the same hospitality that is due every baptized Catholic. So although there was a time when such a union was seen as less than desirable–a compromise which would not bear fruit, a cross and burden for all to bear–today the Church's prayer and hope echoes Jesus' "May they be one in us, Father, as you are in me and I in you."

The experience of "oneness" in an interfaith marriage is still an endeavor of love that takes a lot of work. Yet the Church encourages her children to strive toward that unity as best as they are able. Through the grace of the Sacrament, through shared prayer and love, you can come to know the Love with which the Father loves Jesus; you can come to know that intimacy of body and spirit which is modeled after Jesus' own love for his bride, the Church.

In an interfaith marriage the Church offers guidelines for the rearing of children. This is not done to complicate the marriage, but to keep all things in the light. It would be very easy for two people of different faiths to lose touch with their religions because they do not want to deal with the question of their child's religion. In order to avoid any difficulties after the marriage, the Church asks the couple to discuss and decide the question of the children's religion *before* the marriage.

It is easy for two engaged people to accept the fact of each other's religious persuasion as adults, but you must also plan and prepare for your child's. Do not put off this decision; confront it head on during the time of courtship, lest an unnecessary crisis arise later.

On pages 18–21, above, the guidelines for interfaith marriages are further explained. Use them for reference as you and your fiancé(e) face your differences now, with love.

Six

INTRODUCTION

There are many details that must be checked and rechecked in preparing for your wedding. In the pages that follow, the author has tried to put them into handy checklists and order them with some precision. The lists are by no means complete; everyone has that extra special item or activity that can be added. You may add yours into this compilation in the extra spaces provided.*

To help you keep an eye on things at a glance, you should keep a large calendar on your door. In this way you can write in all the necessary calls and appointments that must be taken care of. The checklists below provide spaces for dates and phone numbers. By using these, you can carry all the information you need with you as you go about town preparing for the celebration.

Regarding the etiquette expected for such a day, some general observations can be made. Details, however, are better left to the "experts" whose books are listed below. Since these are only for reference, you might consider borrowing them from the library:

Letitia Baldrige. Letitia Baldrige's Complete Guide to The New Manners for the '90s. New York, NY: Rawson Associates Macmillan Publishing Company, 1990.

---

*Suggestions regarding additions to these lists from readers would be welcomed by the author for possible inclusion in later revisions of this book. They may be sent to the author through the publisher, Crossroad Publishing Company, 370 Lexington Avenue, New York, NY 10017.

Judith Martin. *Miss Manners on {Painfully Proper} Weddings*. New York, NY: Crown Publishers, Inc., 1995.

Elizabeth L. Post. *Emily Post's Complete Book of Wedding Etiquette.* Revised edition. New York, NY: Harper Collins Publishers, 1991.

EXPENSES: WHO PAYS FOR WHAT?

Traditionally, the bride's family is responsible for the cost of a wedding, although more and more couples are beginning to assume all or part of this responsibility themselves. You and your fiancé(e) should decide in the beginning which approach is best for you. Then notify everyone concerned of your decision, making sure that you are specific. This will eliminate the possibility of any misunderstanding when it comes time for the bills to be paid.

Unless otherwise determined, the groom should assume responsibility for paying the following: the bride's wedding ring, a keepsake for each usher and the best man, the honeymoon, the fee for the clergyman (this may be included in the fee or stipend for the Church, which the bride should offer to pay), tips for the altar servers (if any), as well as the flowers used by the wedding party—the bride's bouquet, her going-away corsage, corsages for the mothers, the boutonnieres for himself, his best man, and the ushers. Other expenses are assumed by the bride's family. As per *Emily Post's Complete Book of Wedding Etiquette,* these are:

Engraved invitations and announcements, and mailing costs

Bridal outfit, and the bridal attendants' dresses, if they cannot afford to pay for them

Bridal and wedding photographs

Bridal consultant and social secretary, if needed

Bride's trousseau

Household trousseau

Cost of bride's premarital blood test for wedding license

Wedding reception

Flowers for the church and reception, as well as for wedding attendants

Gifts for bridal attendants

Groom's wedding ring, if any

Music at the church (including organist and choir) and at the reception

Sexton's fee (church fee)

Carpets, ribbons, awnings, tents–anything rented for the wedding or reception

Gratuities for off-duty policemen or others directing traffic and parking at either the church or reception

Transportation for the bridal party from house to ceremony and from ceremony to reception

A wedding gift of substance or a honeymoon trip

Hotel bills for out-of-town attendants when they can't be accommodated in friends' homes

SEATING IN THE CHURCH

The bride's family sits on the left side of the church, while the groom's family sits on the right.

The groom's mother is the next to last to be seated. She is escorted to the first pew on the right side by the head usher, or her son should he be a member of the wedding party. The groom's father follows several steps behind.

The bride's mother is the last person to be seated before the processional starts. She is escorted to the first pew on the left-hand side by the head usher, or her son should he be a member of the wedding party. After giving the bride away, the father of the bride should sit with his wife.

DIVORCED AND/OR SEPARATED PARENTS

It is only proper that at your wedding, your divorced and/or separated parents resolve to put aside their differences and control their personal feelings, in order to keep everyone's focus on the bride and groom. There are several guidelines to follow in these cases, but they all boil down to one: It is *your* wedding and should not be disrupted or diminished because of the unfortunate relationship between your parents.

SEATING IN THE CHURCH WHEN PARENTS ARE DIVORCED AND/OR SEPARATED

The mother of the bride sits in the first pew on the left. If she has remarried, her husband should be seated in the same pew but ahead of time. If she has not remarried, she should sit alone or invite a close relative to sit with her.

After giving the bride away, the father of the bride should sit in the second or third pew on the left with his parents or his wife, if she attends.

The above seating plan also applies to the groom's parents should they be divorced or separated.

CHECKLIST ONE: THE COUPLE'S CALENDAR

Checklist One offers a suggested schedule that might help in your preparations for a completely traditional wedding. Space has been left at the end of each section so that any special details may be included. Please note that the advance timing suggested for some arrangements may vary, especially in the selection of church and reception facilities.

SIX TO NINE MONTHS BEFORE WEDDING

1. Discuss with your fiancé(e) the style or type of wedding you want, what your budget is, how many guests you want to have, how expenses will be handled, etc.
2. Choose the date of the wedding, the church or place of worship in which the ceremony will be held, and the place for the reception.
3. See your priest. Set dates for Pre-Cana instruction.
4. Plan color scheme for ceremony and reception.
5. Choose and order wedding attire and accessories for both bride and groom and for the attendants.
6. Begin to work on guest list. Both sets of parents should be consulted for this. Ask them to list their guests on 3 × 5 index cards, for easy filing and reference.
7. Decide on your china and silver patterns.
8. Purchase a record book for keeping track of the names and addresses of those who have given you gifts.
9. Set dates for apartment/house hunting. Look for furnishings.
10. Discuss honeymoon. Begin to plan arrangements, e.g., passports, reservations, etc.

11. Start considering music for the reception.

12. Contact florist, photographer, and limousine service, if necessary, for transportation of all members of the wedding party to the church.

THREE MONTHS BEFORE WEDDING

1. Finish guest list.
2. Order invitations and announcements. Remember to order extra envelopes. See if stationer will give outer envelopes to you ahead of time. Begin addressing these as soon as they arrive.
3. Bride shops for trousseau.
4. If bride has ordered her gown, check for delivery date.
5. Begin to plan religious ceremony.
6. Start thinking of gifts for attendants and a gift for your fiancé(e).
7. Begin to shop for wedding rings.
8. If the bride intends to have her photograph placed in a newspaper announcement of the wedding, arrangements for a studio portrait should begin now. It takes time to have the film processed, selected, etc. Editors require an 8 × 10 black and white glossy print.
9. Start working on Marriage Booklet (see pages 28–29, 158–75).

ONE MONTH BEFORE WEDDING

1. Purchase necessary gifts for fiancé(e) and attendants.
2. Mail invitations.
3. Have wedding gowns and suits fitted.
4. Order rings.
5. Arrange for accommodations for attendants from out

of town. This may have to be done earlier if the wedding is to take place in a resort area that has a busy season.

6. Plan rehearsal dinner.

7. Begin preparations for bridesmaids' luncheon or groom's bachelor dinner, if they are to be given.

8. Begin writing thank-you notes for gifts already received. *It is important that you do not fall behind with this.*

9. Prepare announcement for newspapers. Most editors require the information, plus photograph, at least two weeks in advance of the day you want it to appear.

10. Notify the appropriate authorities of forthcoming name changes, if any, on Social Security cards, driver's licenses, credit cards, insurance policies, etc.

11. Make new wills.

12. Purchase honeymoon luggage if needed.

13. Obtain marriage license and take blood tests if necessary. Since blood test results and/or the license may take over a week, it is best to get this done now. Contact your state authorities regarding their requirements; the states vary.

TWO WEEKS BEFORE WEDDING

1. Make arrangements with hairdresser/barber.
2. Check on transportation for the wedding party to the church.
3. Look into possible purchase of floater insurance policy for gifts.
4. Finalize rehearsal time.

ONE WEEK BEFORE WEDDING

REMEMBER TO STAY CALM. IT WILL ALL WORK OUT!

1. Begin honeymoon packing.
2. Finish addressing announcements. These should be

mailed the day of the wedding; entrust that job to an attendant or friend.

3. Confirm number of reception guests with reception facility.

4. Make final check with florist, photographer, musicians, etc.

5. Begin to move belongings to new place of residence. (N.B.: Some couples start doing this over the previous few weeks. Sometimes either the bride or the groom has already moved into the apartment. A great deal depends on each individual situation.)

6. Keep on writing your thank-you notes.

7. Arrange for a table to display your gifts at the reception. (Before the wedding, arrange to have someone stay wherever the wedding gifts are being stored.)

8. Prepare a guest book for the reception. Make sure that pens are available and that someone will be stationed nearby so that your guests know that they should sign in.

9. Custom has it that the bride will need "something old, something new, something borrowed, something blue." Make the appropriate arrangements for these at this time.

10. Decide on the receiving line. A traditional line comprises the following:

Mother of the bride
Father of the groom (optional)
Mother of the groom
Father of the bride (optional)
Bride
Groom
Maid or matron of honor
Bridesmaids

Should either set of parents be divorced or separated, the above order may still be followed, except that the new husband or wife is not part of the receiving line.

CHECKLIST TWO: THE CHURCH

NAME OF THE CHURCH

______________________________ PHONE #__________

ADDRESS

____

CLERGYMAN

____

DATE CHOSEN______ TIME______

MASS______ CEREMONY______

PRE-CANA COUPLE

______________________________ PHONE #__________

DATES FOR PRE-CANA__________

REHEARSAL TIME__________

REHEARSAL DATE__________

ORGANIST

______________________________ PHONE #__________

SINGER

______________________________ PHONE #__________

FEE FOR CHURCH $__________ DATE DUE__________

FEE FOR ORGANIST $__________* DATE DUE__________

* In some parishes, this fee must be paid even if you use your own singer, organist, or other musician, rather than the church's.

FEE FOR SINGER $______________* DATE DUE__________

FEE FOR MUSICIAN(S) $________* DATE DUE__________

TIP FOR ALTAR
SERVERS (IF ANY) $____________ (Usually given on wedding date itself)

____

____

CHECKLIST THREE: PREPARATION OF THE CHURCH

Banners

DESCRIBE

____

WHERE ARE THEY HUNG

____

PERSON RESPONSIBLE

__________________________ PHONE #__________

Flowers

HOW MANY GROUPINGS

____

WHERE ARE THEY LOCATED

____

WHEN ARE THEY DUE

____

FLORIST

__________________________ PHONE #__________

Offertory gifts

WHERE ARE THEY LOCATED

____

PERSON RESPONSIBLE

________________________ PHONE #__________

ITEMS TO BE USED

Bread and wine__________ Cruets__________

Chalice__________ Sacramentary__________

Ciboria__________ Other__________

Printed booklets

PERSON RESPONSIBLE

________________________ PHONE #__________

Miscellaneous

PERSON RESPONSIBLE FOR:

runner__________________________

microphone__________________________

music stands__________________________

candles and placement of
candles for lighting of the
wedding candle ceremony__________________

name cards for special seats__________________

seating arrangements__________________

____

____

CHECKLIST FOUR: PEOPLE IN ATTENDANCE

Best man

NAME____________________ PHONE #________

Maid/Matron of honor

NAME____________________ PHONE #________

Other attendants (both men and women may usher; make sure they know any special seating)

NAME____________________ PHONE #________

NAME____________________ PHONE #________

NAME____________________ PHONE #________

NAME____________________ PHONE #________

NAME____________________ PHONE #________

NAME____________________ PHONE #________

Lectors (number depends on the readings chosen)

NAME____________________ PHONE #________

NAME____________________ PHONE #________

NAME____________________ PHONE #________

Altar servers (usually assigned by the priest; check to be sure)

NAME____________________ PHONE #________

NAME________________________ PHONE #__________

NAME________________________ PHONE #__________

Singer

NAME________________________ PHONE #__________

Organist

NAME________________________ PHONE #__________

Other musicians

NAME________________________ PHONE #__________

NAME________________________ PHONE #__________

NAME________________________ PHONE #__________

Deacon

NAME________________________ PHONE #__________

Presider and concelebrants

NAME________________________ PHONE #__________

NAME________________________ PHONE #__________

NAME________________________ PHONE #__________

Guest minister or rabbi

NAME________________________ PHONE #__________

____

____

CHECKLIST FIVE: WEDDING DURING MASS

A. ENTRANCE RITE

1. Type of procession (pp. 29 and 36)

   traditional________

   family ________

2. Opening Prayer (pp. 36–38)

   Choose A B C D

B. LITURGY OF THE WORD

Choose two or three Scripture passages. The last one must be from the Gospels (pp. 100–18). Should you choose only two readings, the first can be from either the Old Testament (pp. 58–73) or the New Testament (pp. 80–99). A Responsorial Psalm, prayed or sung, follows this first reading. When three readings are chosen, the second one should be from the New Testament. If an Alleluia Verse is used, it should always be sung before the Gospel.

1. First Reading (pp. 58–73) ________

   READER________________________________

2. Responsorial Psalm (pp. 73–80)________

   READER________________________________

3. Second Reading (pp. 80–99) ________

   READER________________________________

4. Alleluia Verse (p. 100) ________

5. Gospel (pp. 100–18) ________

   Always proclaimed by priest or deacon

C. MARRIAGE RITE

1. Form of consent (pp. 40–42)

   present formula ________

   optional U.S. formula________

2. Vows (pp. 38–42)

   to be questions asked by the priest ________

   to be statements made to each other________

   to be committed to memory ________

   read from a card ________

   repeated after priest ________

3. Blessing and Exchange of Rings (pp. 42–43)

   Choose A B C

   Single ring________ Double ring________

   Exchange of rings

   memorized________

   read ________

   repeated ________

4. Local practices (p. 32)________________________________

   ____

5. General Intercessions (pp. 43–44)

   Prepared by________________________________

   Response will be________________________________

D. LITURGY OF THE EUCHARIST

1. Presentation of Gifts (pp. 45–46)

   procession Yes_______ No_______

   people in procession____________________________

   ____

   ____

   ____

2. Prayer over the Gifts

   (pp. 45–46) Choose A B C

3. Preface (pp. 46–47) Choose A B C
4. Holy, holy, holy Recited_____ Sung_____
5. Eucharistic Prayer

   (p. 48) Choose 1 2 3 4

6. Memorial Acclamation

   (p. 48) Choose 1 2 3 4

   Recited_____ Sung_____

7. Great Amen Recited_____ Sung_____

E. THE COMMUNION RITE

1. Lord's Prayer Recited_____ Sung_____
2. Nuptial Blessing

   (pp. 48–52) Choose A B C

3. Sign of Peace (p. 31 explains any special options

you may want to use at this time. Note them if you intend to use any.) ______________________

____

4. Communion (p. 52) — Both species ______ Host only ______
5. Prayer After Communion (p. 53) — Choose A B C
6. Local practices (p. 32) ______________

____

F. CONCLUDING RITE

Final Blessing (pp. 54–56) Choose A B C D

MUSIC SELECTIONS

1. Before service begins

____

____

____

2. Opening song

____

3. Responsorial Psalm (if sung) ______
4. Alleluia Verse (if sung) ______
5. Song during Marriage Rite

____

6. Offertory Song

____

7. Holy, holy, holy (if sung) ________

8. Memorial Acclamation (if sung) ________

9. The Great Amen (if sung) ________

10. Lamb of God (if sung) ________

11. Communion Song

____

12. Song of Praise after Communion

____

13. Recessional Song

____

14. Recessional

____

15. Post-Recessional music

____

____

____

PRIEST'S COPY
CHECKLIST FIVE

A. ENTRANCE RITE

1. Type of procession (pp. 29 and 36)

   traditional________

   family ________

2. Opening Prayer (pp. 36–38)

   Choose **A** **B** **C** **D**

B. LITURGY OF THE WORD

Choose two or three Scripture passages. The last one must be from the Gospels (pp. 100–18). Should you choose only two readings, the first can be from either the Old Testament (pp. 58–73) or the New Testament (pp. 80–99). A Responsorial Psalm, prayed or sung, follows this first reading. When three readings are chosen, the second one should be from the New Testament. If an Alleluia Verse is used, it should always be sung before the Gospel.

1. First Reading (pp. 58–73) ________

   READER________________________________

2. Responsorial Psalm (pp. 73–80)________

   READER________________________________

3. Second Reading (pp. 80–99) ________

   READER________________________________

4. Alleluia Verse (p. 100) ________

5. Gospel (pp. 100–18) ________

Always proclaimed by priest or deacon

C. MARRIAGE RITE

1. Form of consent (pp. 40–42)

   present formula ________

   optional U.S. formula________

2. Vows (pp. 38–42)

   to be questions asked by the priest ________

   to be statements made to each other________

   to be committed to memory ________

   read from a card ________

   repeated after priest ________

3. Blessing and Exchange of Rings (pp. 42–43)

   Choose A B C

   Single ring________ Double ring________

   Exchange of rings

   memorized________

   read ________

   repeated ________

4. Local practices (p. 32)________________________

   ____

5. General Intercessions (pp. 43–44)

   Prepared by________________________

   Response will be________________________

D. LITURGY OF THE EUCHARIST

1. Presentation of Gifts (pp. 45–46)

   procession Yes________ No________

   people in procession________________________________

   ____

   ____

   ____

2. Prayer over the Gifts

   (pp. 45–46) Choose A B C

3. Preface (pp. 46–47) Choose A B C

4. Holy, holy, holy Recited______ Sung______

5. Eucharistic Prayer

   (p. 48) Choose 1 2 3 4

6. Memorial Acclamation

   (p. 48) Choose 1 2 3 4

   Recited______ Sung______

7. Great Amen Recited______ Sung______

E. THE COMMUNION RITE

1. Lord's Prayer Recited______ Sung______

2. Nuptial Blessing

   (pp. 48–52) Choose A B C

3. Sign of Peace (p. 31 explains any special options

you may want to use at this time. Note them if you intend to use any.) ____________________

____

4. Communion (p. 52) — Both species ________ Host only ________

5. Prayer After Communion (p. 53) — Choose A B C

6. Local practices (p. 32) ____________________

____

F. CONCLUDING RITE

Final Blessing (pp. 54–56) Choose A B C D

MUSIC SELECTIONS

1. Before service begins

____

____

____

2. Opening song

____

3. Responsorial Psalm (if sung) ________

4. Alleluia Verse (if sung) ________

5. Song during Marriage Rite

____

6. Offertory Song

____

7. Holy, holy, holy (if sung) ________
8. Memorial Acclamation (if sung) ________
9. The Great Amen (if sung) ________
10. Lamb of God (if sung) ________
11. Communion Song

____

12. Song of Praise after Communion

____

13. Recessional Song

____

14. Recessional

____

15. Post-Recessional music

____

____

____

CHECKLIST SIX: WEDDING OUTSIDE OF MASS

A. ENTRANCE RITE

1. Type of procession (pp. 29 and 36)

   traditional ________

   family ________

2. Opening Prayer (pp. 36–38)

   Choose: A B C D

B. LITURGY OF THE WORD

Choose two or three Scripture passages. The last one must be from the Gospels (pp. 100–18). Should you choose only two readings, the first can be from either the Old Testament (pp. 58–73) or the New Testament (pp. 80–99). A Responsorial Psalm, prayed or sung, follows this first reading. When three readings are chosen, the second one should be from the New Testament. If an Alleluia Verse is used, it should always be sung before the Gospel.

1. First Reading (pp. 58–73) ________

   READER________________________________

2. Responsorial Psalm (pp. 73–80) ________

   READER________________________________

3. Second Reading (pp. 80–99) ________

   READER________________________________

4. Alleluia Verse (p. 100) ________

5. Gospel (pp. 100–18) ________

   Always proclaimed by priest or deacon

C. MARRIAGE RITE

1. Form of consent (pp. 40–42)

   present formula ________

   optional U.S. formula________

2. Vows (pp. 38–42)

   to be questions asked by the priest ________

   to be statements made to each other________

   to be committed to memory ________

   read from a card ________

   repeated after priest ________

3. Blessing and Exchange of Rings (pp. 42–43)

   Choose A B C

   Single ring________ Double ring________

   Exchange of rings

   memorized________

   read ________

   repeated ________

4. Local practices (p. 32)________________________________

   ____

5. General Intercessions (pp. 43–44)

   Prepared by________________________________

   Response will be____________________________

6. Nuptial Blessing (pp. 48–52) Choose A B C

For the marriage between a Catholic and an unbaptized person, the following Nuptial Blessing is used:

Holy Father, creator of the universe,
maker of man and woman in your likeness,
source of blessing for married life,
we humbly pray to you for this bride
who today is united with her husband in the bond of marriage.
May your fullest blessing come upon her and her husband
so that they may together rejoice in your gift of married love.
May they be noted for their good lives,
(and be persons filled with virtue).
Lord, may they both praise you when they are happy
and turn to you in their sorrows.
May they reach old age in the company of their friends,
and come at last to the Kingdom of heaven.
We ask this through Christ our Lord.
Amen.

D. CONCLUDING RITE

Lord's Prayer (optional) ________

Final Blessing (pp. 54–56) Choose A B C

MUSIC SELECTIONS

1. Before service begins

____

____

____

2. Opening song

____

3. Responsorial Psalm (if sung) ________

4. Alleluia Verse (if sung) ________

5. Song during Marriage Rite (optional)

____

6. Recessional Song

____

7. Recessional

____

8. Post-Recessional music

____

____

____

PRIEST'S COPY
CHECKLIST SIX

A. ENTRANCE RITE

1. Type of procession (pp. 29 and 36)

   traditional________

   family ________

2. Opening Prayer (pp. 36–38)

   Choose: A B C D

B. LITURGY OF THE WORD

Choose two or three Scripture passages. The last one must be from the Gospels (pp. 100–18). Should you choose only two readings, the first can be from either the Old Testament (pp. 58–73) or the New Testament (pp. 80–99). A Responsorial Psalm, prayed or sung, follows this first reading. When three readings are chosen, the second one should be from the New Testament. If an Alleluia Verse is used, it should always be sung before the Gospel.

1. First Reading (pp. 58–73) ________

   READER________________________________

2. Responsorial Psalm (pp. 73–80)________

   READER________________________________

3. Second Reading (pp. 80–99) ________

   READER________________________________

4. Alleluia Verse (p. 100) ________

5. Gospel (pp. 100–18) ________

   Always proclaimed by priest or deacon

C. MARRIAGE RITE

1. Form of consent (pp. 40–42)

   present formula ________

   optional U.S. formula________

2. Vows (pp. 38–42)

   to be questions asked by the priest ________

   to be statements made to each other________

   to be committed to memory ________

   read from a card ________

   repeated after priest ________

3. Blessing and Exchange of Rings (pp. 42–43)

   Choose A B C

   Single ring________ Double ring________

   Exchange of rings

   memorized________

   read ________

   repeated ________

4. Local practices (p. 32)________________________________

   ____

5. General Intercessions (pp. 43–44)

   Prepared by________________________________

   Response will be________________________________

6. Nuptial Blessing (pp. 48–52) Choose A B C

For the marriage between a Catholic and an unbaptized person, the following Nuptial Blessing is used:

Holy Father, creator of the universe,
maker of man and woman in your likeness,
source of blessing for married life,
we humbly pray to you for this bride
who today is united with her husband in the bond of marriage.
May your fullest blessing come upon her and her husband
so that they may together rejoice in your gift of married love.
May they be noted for their good lives,
(and be persons filled with virtue).
Lord, may they both praise you when they are happy
and turn to you in their sorrows.
May they reach old age in the company of their friends,
and come at last to the Kingdom of heaven.
We ask this through Christ our Lord.
Amen.

D. CONCLUDING RITE

Lord's Prayer (optional) ________

Final Blessing (pp. 54–56) Choose A B C

MUSIC SELECTIONS

1. Before service begins

____

____

____

2. Opening song

____

3. Responsorial Psalm (if sung) ________

4. Alleluia Verse (if sung) ________

5. Song during Marriage Rite (optional)

____

6. Recessional Song

____

7. Recessional

____

8. Post-Recessional music

____

____

____

CHECKLIST SEVEN: OTHER NAMES AND PHONE NUMBERS

RECEPTION FACILITY

______________________________ PHONE #__________

ADDRESS

____

MANAGER____

MUSICIANS FOR RECEPTION

______________________________ PHONE #__________

______________________________ PHONE #__________

PHOTOGRAPHER

______________________________ PHONE #__________

FLORIST

______________________________ PHONE #__________

ADDRESS

____

SALESPERSON______________________________________

BRIDAL SHOP

______________________________ PHONE #__________

ADDRESS

____

SALESPERSON______________________________________

TUXEDO RENTAL

______________________________ PHONE #__________

ADDRESS

____

SALESPERSON____________________________________

LIMOUSINE SERVICE

______________________________ PHONE #__________

ADDRESS

____

PRINTER FOR BOOKLET

______________________________ PHONE #__________

ADDRESS

____

SALESPERSON____________________________________

PRINTER FOR INVITATIONS

______________________________ PHONE #__________

ADDRESS

____

SALESPERSON____________________________________

PLACE FOR REHEARSAL DINNER

______________________________ PHONE #__________

ADDRESS

____

MANAGER_______________________________________

Appendices

IMPORTANCE AND DIGNITY OF THE SACRAMENT OF MATRIMONY

1. Married Christians, in virtue of the sacrament of matrimony, signify and share in the mystery of that unity and fruitful love which exists between Christ and His Church; they help each other to attain to holiness in their married life and in the rearing and education of their children; and they have their own special gift among the people of God.

2. Marriage arises in the covenant of marriage, or irrevocable consent, which each partner freely bestows on and accepts from the other. This intimate union and the good of the children impose total fidelity on each of them and argue for an unbreakable oneness between them. Christ the Lord raised this union to the dignity of a sacrament so that it might more clearly recall and more easily reflect His own unbreakable union with His Church.

3. Christian couples, therefore, nourish and develop their marriage by undivided affection, which wells up from the fountain of divine love, while, in a merging of human and divine love, they remain faithful in body and in mind, in good times as in bad.

4. By their very nature, the institution of matrimony and wedded love are ordained for the procreation and education of children and find in them their ultimate crown.

Therefore, married Christians, while not considering the other purposes of marriage of less account, should be steadfast and ready to cooperate with the love of the Creator and Savior, who through them will constantly enrich and enlarge His own family.

5. A priest should bear in mind these principles of faith, both in his instructions to those about to be married and when giving the homily during the marriage ceremony. He should relate his instructions to the texts of the sacred readings.

The bridal couple should be given a review of the fundamentals of Christian doctrine. This may include instruction on the teachings about marriage and the family, on the rites used in the celebration of the sacrament itself, and on the prayers and readings. In this way the bridegroom and the bride will receive far greater benefit from the celebration.

6. In the celebration of marriage (which normally should be within the Mass), certain elements should be stressed, especially the Liturgy of the Word, which shows the importance of Christian marriage in the history of salvation and the duties and responsibility of the couple in caring for the holiness of their children. Also of supreme importance are the consent of the contracting parties, which the priest asks and receives; the special Nuptial Blessing for the bride and for the marriage covenant; and finally, the reception of Holy Communion by the groom and the bride, and by all present, by which their love is nourished and all are lifted up into communion with our Lord and with one another.

7. Priests should first of all strengthen and nourish the faith of those about to be married, for the sacrament of matrimony presupposes and demands faith.

–RITE OF MARRIAGE
(Introduction)

COPYRIGHTS

Remember that you cannot reprint, duplicate, or make Xerox copies of the words and/or music notation of a copyrighted song without the permission of the copyright owner. Most companies give this permission automatically and free of charge, provided the following conditions are fulfilled:

Only words are printed in the booklet.

Copies are not sold; remaining copies of the booklet are to be collected and destroyed after using them for the wedding.

Proper copyright notification must be given. This includes the symbol ©, the date, and the copyright owner. An example of this form appears in the sample booklet on page 173.

Copyright owner must be informed of the songs printed and the number of booklets made.

Some companies may charge a fee. This is usually quite small and should pose little problem for any couple. You must check with each company for specific details. A partial listing of some popular music companies follows:

EMI Christian Music Publishing, Inc., 101 Winers Circle/PO Box 5085, Brentwood, TN 37024-5085. Phone: 615-371-4400.

F.E.L Publications, Ltd., now assigned to Lorenz Corporation, PO Box 802, Dayton, OH 45401-0802. Phone: 513-228-6118.

G.I.A. Publications, Inc., 7404 So. Mason Ave., Chicago, IL 60638.

Integrity's Hosanna! Music, administered by Integrity, Inc., PO Box 851622, Mobile, AL 36685-1622. Phone: 334-633-9000.

Maranatha Music, administered by The Copyright Company, 40 Music Square East, Nashville, TN 37203. Phone: 615-244-5588.

NALR (North American Liturgy Resources) copyrights are now owned and administered by OCP Publications.

Oregon Catholic Press (OCP), PO Box 18030, Portland, OR 97218-0030. Phone: 800-548-8749.

Raven Music, PO Box 77011, Seattle, WA 98177. Phone: 206-367-0736.

Resource Publications, Inc., 160 E. Virginia, San Jose, CA 95112.

Steubenville Liturgical Resources, 745 Brady Ave., Steubenville, OH 43952.

Weston Priory Productions, Weston, VT 05161.

Word Music, 3319 West End Ave., Suite 200, Nashville, TN 37203. Phone: 615-385-9673.

Word of God, PO Box 8617, Ann Arbor, MI 48107.

World Library Publications, PO Box 2701, Schiller Park, IL 60176.

In addition to getting copyright permission for the song lyrics printed in your wedding booklet, you must also print, somewhere in the booklet, the proper copyright notice for any liturgical texts you might print from the ritual, sacramentary, lectionary, etc. This includes prayers and readings. In order to obtain this permission—no royalty is required—write to:

International Committee on English in the Liturgy
1522 K Street, N.W. Suite 1000
Washington, DC 20005-1202
Telephone: 1-202-347-6640.

BOOKLETS

When preparing a booklet for your guests, keep in mind that every prayer and every movement does not need to be printed. The purpose of the booklet is to assist your guests as they join with you in the celebration.

If you are celebrating your wedding within a Nuptial Mass and many of your guests are not Catholic, you may have to put the people's responses into the booklet. The sample booklet at the end of this Appendix takes such an approach. This was done in order to show you the entire flow of the Nuptial Mass and to help you in arranging the information in the proper context. You, however, may include as much or as little as you want, depending on the needs of the congregation.

The easiest way to prepare the booklet for the printer is to use a desktop publishing program. In doing so, it will help if you sketch out a dummy copy to insure correct spacing. For the booklet cover, consider using one of the many clipart images available in most desktop publishing programs, or use a premade cover purchased from a religious supply store. A listing of such stores can be found in your local phone directory.

If you choose to print such a booklet, make sure that you take it to the printer (or place where the duplicating process is to be done) well in advance of the wedding (approximately one month). Before doing so, however, you should have it reread by the priest and music director whom you are consulting about the wedding (see pages 28–29).

In the sample booklet that follows, the numbers in the columns correspond to the page(s) in *Your Catholic Wedding* which refer(s) to that part of the wedding celebration.

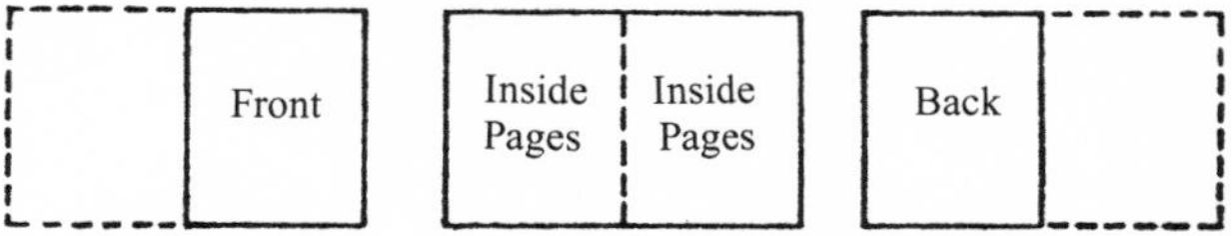

(booklet cover)

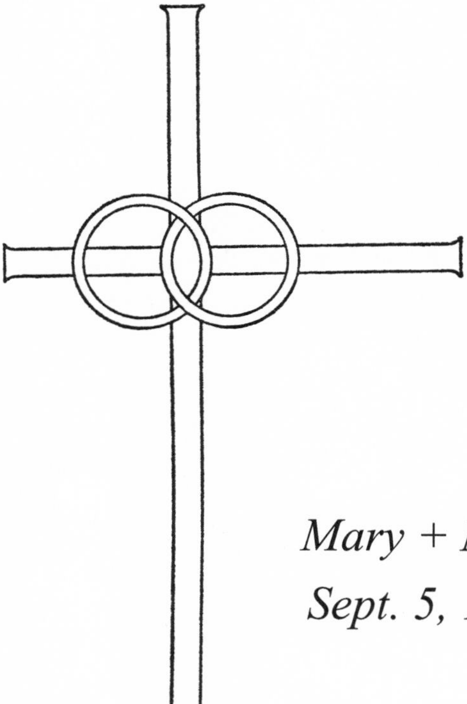

Mary + Mark

Sept. 5, 1997

(inside fr. cover)

At this time we would like to take the time to thank those who made this day a beautiful one for us.

Our parents, whose love and understanding have been a source of joy and support for us in planning this day, and in planning our life as husband and wife.

Our brothers and sisters who were always there when we needed them—especially for those "unexpected" errands—with love and affection.

Our relatives and friends, some of whom had to travel a great distance to be here with us.

A special thank you to our Bridal Party for all the help they gave us in making this day the most important one of our lives.

We love you all,

Mary & Marc

(inside)

NUPTIAL CELEBRATION
of
Mary C. Lenz
and
Marc E. Wieman

Maid of Honor
Tess Prasnikar

Best Man
Bob Farrell

Bridesmaids
Vicki Ouska
Valerie Vetere
Janine Wieman

Ushers
Tom Lenz
Chris Wieman
Eric Wieman

Celebrants
Rev. John Tapper
Rev. James Hart

Lectors
Carol and Lionel Lenz
Karl Wieman

September 5, 1981

Our Lady of the Wayside
Arlington Heights, Illinois

(inside)

PRELUDES "Jesus Joy of Man's Desiring"–Bach
(see p. 26) "Joyful, Joyful We Adore Thee"
–Beethoven

PROCESSIONAL "Trumpet Voluntary in D Major"
(see p. 29) –Purcell

GREETING AND OPENING PRAYER (stand)
(see p. 36)

Priest: Father,
you have made the bond of marriage
a holy mystery,
a symbol of Christ's love for his Church.
Hear our prayers for Marc and Mary.
With faith in you and in each other
they pledge their love today.
May their lives always bear witness
to the reality of that love.

We ask this through our Lord Jesus Christ, your Son, who lives and reigns with you and the Holy Spirit, one God, for ever and ever.

ALL: AMEN.

LITURGY OF THE WORD

FIRST READING Genesis 1:26–28, 31a (sit)
(see pp. 58–73, 80–99)

Lector: God said, "Let us make man in our own image, in the likeness of ourselves, and let them be masters of the fish of the sea, the birds of heaven, the cattle, all the wild beasts and all the reptiles that crawl upon the earth."

(inside)

God created man in the image of himself,
in the image of God he created him,
male and female he created them.

God blessed them, saying to them, "Be fruitful, multiply, fill the earth and conquer it. Be masters of the fish, the birds of heaven and all living animals on the earth."

God saw all he had made, and indeed it was very good.

The Gospel of the Lord.

ALL: THANKS BE TO GOD.

RESPONSORIAL PSALM
(see pp. 73–80)

Lector: The earth is full of the goodness of the Lord.

ALL: THE EARTH IS FULL OF THE GOODNESS OF THE LORD.

Lector: Happy the nation whose God is Yahweh,
the people he has chosen for his heritage.
But see how the eye of Yahweh is on those who fear him,
on those who rely on his love.

ALL: THE EARTH IS FULL OF THE GOODNESS OF THE LORD.

Lector: Our soul awaits Yahweh,
he is our help and shield;
our hearts rejoice in him,
we trust in his holy name.

ALL: THE EARTH IS FULL OF THE GOODNESS OF THE LORD.

Lector: Yahweh, let your love rest on us
as our hope has rested in you.

ALL: THE EARTH IS FULL OF THE GOODNESS OF THE LORD.

(inside)

ALLELUIA VERSE (stand)
(see p. 100)

Singer: Alleluia.
ALL: ALLELUIA.
Singer: Everyone who loves is born of God and knows him.
ALL: ALLELUIA.

GOSPEL Matthew 5:13–16
(see pp. 100–18)

Priest: The Lord be with you.
ALL: AND ALSO WITH YOU.
Priest: A reading from the holy Gospel according to Matthew.
ALL: GLORY TO YOU, LORD.

Jesus said to his disciples:
"You are the salt of the earth. But if salt becomes tasteless, what can make it salty again? It is good for nothing, and can only be thrown out to be trampled underfoot by men.
"You are the light of the world. A city built on a hilltop cannot be hidden. No one lights a lamp to put it under a tub; they put it on the lampstand where it shines for everyone in the house. In the same way your light must shine in the sight of men, so that, seeing your good works, they may give the praise to your Father in heaven."
The Gospel of the Lord.

ALL: PRAISE TO YOU, LORD JESUS CHRIST.

HOMILY (sit)

Guests may remain seated
during the Rite of Marriage

(inside)

EXCHANGE OF VOWS AND BLESSING OF RINGS
(see pp. 40–43)

Priest: Lord,
bless ✠ and consecrate Marc and Mary
in their love for each other.
May these rings be a symbol
of true faith in each other,
and always remind them of their love.

We ask this through Christ our Lord.

ALL: AMEN.

GENERAL INTERCESSIONS (stand)
(see pp. 30 and 43–44)

Priest: Heavenly Father, we gather here today to celebrate the marriage of Marc and Mary. We know our brokenness and our needs, none of which can be healed without your love. And so, confident of your care and concern we pray.

Lector: We pray for your people, your Church. Let her always be a source of light and strength for the married couples in her midst. For this we pray to the Lord.

ALL: LORD, HEAR OUR PRAYER.

Lector: We pray for your people joined in celebration this happy day. Strengthen our resolve to love you and each other with greater depth and sincerity. For this we pray to the Lord.

ALL: LORD, HEAR OUR PRAYER.

Lector: We pray for Marc and Mary. Unite them through the grace of your Holy Spirit so they may be chan-

(inside)

nels of grace for one another and for your people. For this we pray to the Lord.

ALL: LORD, HEAR OUR PRAYER.

Lector: We pray for those who are ill, especially those whose illness comes from the poverty that surrounds them. Grant them your healing strength by sending them believers who will minister to their physical needs. For this we pray to the Lord.

ALL: LORD, HEAR OUR PRAYER.

Lector: We pray for those who have died (pause for silent prayer). Grant them peace in your kingdom. For this we pray to the Lord.

ALL: LORD, HEAR OUR PRAYER.

Priest: Loving Father, we place our lives in your hands, confident that you will always be our strength and protection. We ask this through Christ the Lord.

ALL: AMEN.

LITURGY OF THE EUCHARIST

PRESENTATION OF THE GIFTS (sit)
(see pp. 30–31)

Grandma Reilly
Grandma and Grandpa Lenz
Victoria and Valerie Wieman
will represent us in bringing the gifts to the altar

OFFERTORY SONG "Bless your people, Lord"—Sexton
(see pp. 26–27 and 157) (sit)

ALL: BLESS YOUR PEOPLE, LORD;
GATHER US TOGETHER

(inside)

AS WE STAND AROUND THE TABLE OF YOUR LOVE.

(Verses sung by cantor)

Copyright © 1979 Pat Sexton & Aslan Records, Inc.

Priest: Pray, brethren, that our sacrifice may be acceptable to God, the Almighty Father.

ALL: MAY THE LORD ACCEPT THE SACRIFICE AT YOUR HANDS
FOR THE PRAISE AND GLORY OF HIS NAME,
FOR OUR GOOD, AND THE GOOD OF ALL HIS CHURCH.

PRAYER OVER THE GIFTS
(see pp. 45–46)

Priest: Lord,
accept the gifts we offer you
on this happy day.
In your fatherly love
watch over and protect Marc and Mary,
whom you have united in marriage.

We ask this through Christ our Lord.

ALL: AMEN.

PREFACE (stand)
(see pp. 46–47)

Priest: The Lord be with you.
ALL: AND ALSO WITH YOU.
Priest: Lift up your hearts.
ALL: WE LIFT THEM UP TO THE LORD.
Priest: Let us give thanks to the Lord our God.
ALL: IT IS RIGHT TO GIVE HIM THANKS AND PRAISE.

(inside)

Priest: Father, all-powerful and ever-living God,
we do well always and everywhere to give you thanks.

You created man in love to share your divine life.
We see his high destiny in the love of husband and wife,
which bears the imprint of your own divine love.

Love is man's origin,
love is his constant calling,
love is his fulfillment in heaven.

The love of man and woman
is made holy in the sacrament of marriage,
and becomes the mirror of your everlasting love.

Through Christ the choirs of angels
and all the saints
praise and worship your glory.
May our voices blend with theirs
as we join in their unending hymn:

ALL: HOLY, HOLY, HOLY LORD, GOD OF POWER AND MIGHT, HEAVEN AND EARTH ARE FULL OF YOUR GLORY.
HOSANNA IN THE HIGHEST.
BLESSED IS HE WHO COMES IN THE NAME OF THE LORD.
HOSANNA IN THE HIGHEST.

MEMORIAL ACCLAMATION (kneel)
(see p. 48)

ALL: CHRIST HAS DIED,
CHRIST IS RISEN,
CHRIST WILL COME AGAIN.

(inside)

NUPTIAL BLESSING **(stand)**
(see pp. 48–52)

Priest: My dear friends, let us ask God
for his continued blessings upon Marc and Mary.

Holy Father, creator of the universe,
maker of man and woman in your own likeness,
source of blessing for married life,
we humbly pray to you for this woman
who today is united with her husband in this sacrament of marriage.
May your fullest blessing come upon her and her husband
so that they may together rejoice in your gift of married love
and enrich your Church with their children.

Lord, may they both praise you when they are happy
and turn to you in their sorrows.
May they be glad that you help them in their work
and know that you are with them in their need.
May they pray to you in the community of the Church,
and be your witnesses in the world.
May they reach old age in the company of their friends,
and come at last to the kingdom of heaven.

We ask this through Christ our Lord.

ALL: AMEN.

(inside)

SIGN OF PEACE
(see p. 31)

Priest: Lord Jesus Christ,
you said to your apostles:
I leave you peace, my peace I give you.
Look not on our sins, but on the faith of your Church,
and grant us the peace and unity of your kingdom
where you live for ever and ever.
ALL: AMEN.
Priest: The peace of the Lord be with you always.
ALL: AND ALSO WITH YOU.

LAMB OF GOD

ALL: LAMB OF GOD, YOU TAKE AWAY THE SINS OF THE WORLD:
HAVE MERCY ON US.
LAMB OF GOD, YOU TAKE AWAY THE SINS OF THE WORLD:
HAVE MERCY ON US.
LAMB OF GOD, YOU TAKE AWAY THE SINS OF THE WORLD:
GRANT US PEACE. (kneel)
Priest: This is the Lamb of God
who takes away the sins of the world.
Happy are those who are called to his supper.
ALL: LORD, I AM NOT WORTHY TO RECEIVE YOU,
BUT ONLY SAY THE WORD AND I SHALL BE HEALED.

(inside)

COMMUNION SONG "Pray, People, Pray"—Sexton

Pray, people, pray.
Pray for the house you live in,
and pray for those without a home.
Pray, people, pray.
Pray for the people in it,
and pray for people all alone.

Refrain:
Pray in good times, pray in bad times;
when you're warm or when you're cold.
Pray that you will be delivered from all harm
in younger days till days you're growing old.

Pray, people, pray.
Pray for the gift of wisdom,
and pray for hearts that never die.
Pray, people, pray.
Pray that you'll be forgiven
for all the times you let go by.

Refrain

Pray, people, pray.
Pray for the lives you're given,
and pray for those who waste their lives.
Pray, people, pray.
Pray for the times you live in, and
pray for love . . . pray for peace . . .
Pray, people, pray.

(inside)

LIGHTING OF THE WEDDING CANDLE (sit)
(see pp. 32–33)

By lighting the wedding candle, which symbolizes Christ, Marc and Mary wish to symbolize the ending of two separate lives and their union into one.

MEDITATION SONG "The Canticle"—Aridas

PRAYER AFTER COMMUNION (stand)
(see p. 53)

Priest: Almighty God,
may the sacrifice we have offered
and the Eucharist we have shared
strengthen the love of Marc and Mary,
and give us all your fatherly aid.

We ask this through Christ our Lord.

ALL: AMEN.

FINAL BLESSING
(see pp. 54–56)

Priest: May the Lord Jesus, who was a guest at the wedding in Cana,
bless you and your families and friends.

ALL: AMEN.

Priest: May Jesus, who loved his Church to the end,
always fill your hearts with his love.

ALL: AMEN.

Priest: May he grant that, as you believe in his resurrection,
so you may wait for him in joy and hope.

ALL: AMEN.

Priest: And may almighty God bless you all,
the Father, and the Son, ✠ and the Holy Spirit.

ALL: AMEN.

(inside)

RECESSIONAL SONG "Amen"–Sexton

We have come here, Lord, to do your will now, Lord.
One in voice we sing to you: make us one in mind and heart.
Take us as we are, O Lord, help us on our way.
One in voice we sing to you; bind us as we pray.
Amen. We sing to you, Amen.
Your will be done, our hearts be one. Amen.
Amen. We live for you, Amen.
Your love be here, your peace be near. Amen.
Take our hearts of stone, Lord, and change them with your love.
Fill them with the word, O Lord, of life we're singing of.
When our world is cold and grey fill it with your song.
Songs of peace sung day by day for all to sing along.
Refrain

RECESSIONAL "Trumpet Tune in C Major"–Purcell

COPYRIGHT ACKNOWLEDGMENTS

(see pp. 157–58)

(back of booklet)